Why Christians can't be Democrats
God is the Source, Man is the Force

Michael DeLance Thomas

Michael,

I Hope you enjoy!
To Liberty!

M. _____ 5-11-12

www.whychristianscantbedemocrats.com

Harry Tubman Publishing

Why Christians can't be Democrats

Copyright © 2012 by Harry Tubman publishing

Cover by: Michael DeLance Thomas & Ryan Ellis

Published in the United States by Harry Tubman Publishing

ISBN 978-0-9850288-0-0

Website: www.whychristianscantbedemocrats.com

Email: info@whychristianscantbedemocrats.com

Printed in U.S.A

Fannie Thomas
Thank you for your motivation, input and support

Dan Giannini
Thank you for the coffee shop meetings and advice

Geralmy Swint
Richard Gruetter
Carla Wallace
Tatiana Thorpe
Shannon Wroten
Renece Thomas
Joe White
Torion Kent
Gwenette Moore
Shawn Jeanpierre
Thank you all for your input and support

CONTENTS

GOD IS THE SOURCE

G OD IS THE "SOURCE" OF ALL THINGS THAT ARE GOOD.

H E IS OUR C REATOR

H E IS THE F ATHER

H E IS OUR P ROVIDER

H E IS OUR S ECURITY

H E IS OUR S TRENGTH

H E IS OUR H EALER

H E IS OUR A BUNDANCE

H E IS OUR I NDEPENDENCE

H E IS L OVE

HE IS THE SOURCE!

BEFORE YOU BEGIN

Before you begin reading "Why Christians can't be Democrats," please take a few minutes to jot down, on a physical piece of paper, what God and Christ personally represent to you. Write down what God has done for you. When you think of God and Christ, what comes to mind? Please write that down too. To better understand why Christians can't be Democrats, it is absolutely essential that you perform this step! When you are done, use this list as a bookmark when reading this book. At any time that you start to doubt the concepts within this book, I ask that you refer to what you have written down and mentally apply it to the current passage. It is my belief that we have been so politically misguided, that our understanding of the relationship between Government and God is severely clouded. It is my hope that this book, along with your list, puts you back on the political track for God. It will take the collective efforts of all "believers" to reverse the current and destructive path of our nation.

MAN IS THE FORCE

CHAPTER 1

BATTLE BETWEEN MAN'S-GOVERNMENT & GOD'S-GOVERNMENT

"The only thing necessary for evil to triumph is for good men to do nothing" ~ Sir Edmund Burke

My fellow Christian, we are deep within an ongoing battle. This battle has been going on since the beginning of time and will continue well into the future. It is a battle that most have purposely ignored or simply have not noticed. Millions have died fighting this battle, with most victims not even aware that it existed. It is a battle of Man's-government vs. God's-government. It is for the position of governing and ruling over mankind. Now, considering that God created Man, it appears that God could decide the outcome of this battle at any time. However, it is not His battle to fight - it is ours. We must decide the outcome. It is a battle that continues to be waged and is ever-present. This book serves to educate you on how to recognize the differences between Man's-government and God's-government, so that you may identify each and align yourself with the correct side. History teaches us that Men have been on a constant quest to rule above all others. Like other religions, Christianity is being manipulated, emotionally and politically, for this purpose. Christian values are being destroyed right beneath our noses, but we are too busy living our lives to take notice. Therefore, we are engaged within a battle, but more defenseless than ever before.

As you read this book, I ask that you set aside your biases, clear your heart, and suspend any Christian arrogance you may have, so that you can align yourself on the side with God in the war of all wars; a war between good and evil; a war between love and hate; a war between freedom and enslavement; a war between God's-government and Man's-government. Over time, our nation has shifted towards the very thing that prior generations have fought and died against - centralized enslavement under the rule of Man. We have misquoted things so much that they have become the accepted truth. Too many Christians have unknowingly placed themselves in an inferior position with Men as our masters, rather than the Master Himself. History has proven that all previous civilizations that adopted a huge reliance upon Man's-government have collapsed. Simply, fallible and imperfect men cannot save other fallible and imperfect men. Men are not and cannot be the saviors of other men, yet we continue to put our faith into Man's-government to do so, while at the same time claiming that same faith within God.

The purpose of this book is not to educate you on politics, Christianity or religion, nor debate scripture interpretation or political talking points. It is an examination on the concept of government - what government is and is not. After reading this book, I strongly encourage you to include the discussion of God's-government and Man's-government part of your bible study. That is to say, educating yourself only on the ways of God while ignoring the discussion of Man's-government is a sure way to subject yourself to enslavement under the rule of Man. God's-government and Man's-government have a union and that union is critical in obtaining liberty. One requires the other, but God's-government must always remain far more superior between the two. Unfortunately, we have been taught and encouraged to separate the union between the two. This has either been done out of ignorance or for personal gain. Regarding the latter, there are those who aspire to rule over you and they understand that you cannot serve two Masters. You cannot equally serve both them (Man's-government) and God (God's-government). Therefore, they must first separate you from God and the things of God, if they are to ever gain His throne. Before going any further, understand that this book is not an "anti-government rant." There is a legitimate place for Man's-government in society. It plays an essential role in our freedoms, but it should always remain small and kept on a very short leash.

I encourage you to take the time and reflect upon the philosophies within this book. In doing so, I ask that you be intellectually honest with yourself, your Christian beliefs and faith. We have ignored God principles or allowed our emotions to mask them. Over time, we have been programmed to look beyond reality (i.e. those principles found within nature) and accept only those things that "appear" to be good and of God. It is my goal to expose that although the ideology of the Democrat Party may attempt to align itself with Christ and God's-government, its methods are quite the opposite of both. As Christians, we must not only recognize the things of God, but also equally understand those things that are not. Although the philosophies and theories within this book could be applied to any existing political party, the focus will be on the two major ones - the Democrats and the Republicans. This is because our country needs to make a fundamental shift in political policy, if we are to save our Republic from collapse. Until we have a third, serious contender, chances are that future positions in Government will most likely come out of these two parties.

Before going further, let me be very clear - as a whole, I do not consider the Democrat Party an enemy of God, nor necessarily the people within it. The party is comprised of wonderful people with socially noble causes. Conversely, I do not believe that the Republican Party, as a whole, is a friend of God, nor necessarily all of the people within it. Neither party is without its faults. This book is not about tearing down one party or person in order to build up another. There will be no name-calling or the blame game played here. This book is simply about examining how the overall ideologies of two parties align with the "methods" of Christ. It is through this examination that will give us a better idea of the path that we need to be on to restore our nation to "one nation under God." It is not my purpose to absolutely demand where Christians should be politically, but to warn where we should not be. Now, no one reading this book can say with one hundred percent certainty that they personally know Christ more or better than anyone else. Thus, it is not my intention to challenge specific scripture or its various interpretations or perceptions. That would be a waste of time, considering it is exactly the reason that we have so many different religious denominations now. If you are looking for such a fight, you will not find it here. The approach will be a philosophical one, based on shared tenets throughout denominations. I will not debate specifics, but rather expose commonly agreed-upon generalizations. The philosophical approach will be based on what Christ represented and the methods He used to support those values. Some of the biggest hurdles ahead will be your perception of our roles as Christians, your current viewpoints on the Democrat and Republican parties, your emotions and misinformation you have been given over the years. Those are some mighty big hurdles! I ask that you pray and have an open heart and mind to fully receive and digest this information. I suspect that most people won't finish this book, not because of its contents but because of what may be revealed. My intentions are not to examine and scrutinize, but simply to expose those things not of Christ. I ask that you look in the mirror and question your actions as a Christian, not what you claim to be.

This book was written for anyone who wants to improve society and the human condition using the methods of Christ, rather than the methods of Man. It is not meant to divide Christians politically, but to actually yoke us together under the same political umbrella - on the side of God. This book is meant to question your personal responsibilities and accountability when it comes to performing your Christian duties. Understanding the theories within this book do not require a degree in theology, philosophy or political science. They are based upon self-evident principles found throughout God's nature and universe. While reading this book, try clearing your mind of specific names of politicians and political mishaps. Opinions change with understanding. All that is required is an open mind and faith.

CHAPTER 2

TO GOVERN OR NOT TO GOVERN?

"Government is not reason; it is not eloquence. It is force. And force, like fire, is a dangerous servant and a fearful master."
~ George Washington

Govern - to steer (origin Latin/Greek)

Based on the origin of the word, "govern" means "to steer." If you would apply that concept to yourself, you can either choose to steer yourself or be steered by others. In other words, you can either govern yourself or others will govern you. This should be the mind set we take before performing any actions we take as individuals. Each of us must decide if we are going to steer our next course of action or have it determined by others. Are you charting the direction of your life or is it being charted for you?

Ask someone at random what they believe the responsibility or purpose of Government is and you will be amazed by their answer. They will tell you what they believe it is, but chances are they will look to you for confirmation in their answer. This should be a red flag on why society is on the decline. Simply, most people no longer understand, nor respect what has to be one of the greatest dangers to the existence of mankind - Government! It has become so entangled in our lives that it is accepted as if it is another member of the community. For the most part, we have embraced it and invited it into our homes and even or relationships. However, if we knew the underlying dangers of Government, we would immediately reject it and keep it at a distance. What was understood to be a "necessary danger" and kept at a distance by previous generations, Man's-government has found its way of being welcomed with open arms by current-day society. Though we have advanced in knowledge, we seem to be severely lacking in understanding. The underlying morality of society is getting worse because we have literally transferred our God-given power to the politician (Man's-government). As a nation, we tend to idolize presidents more than God. We rejoice when statues idolizing various men and women are erected, but stand silent when displays of Christ are forcefully removed in the name of "fairness." Where we once sought God to provide, Man's-government now provides. Where we once sought God to be our "security net" for life adversities, Man's-government now provides social programs. Where we once sought God for our healing needs, Man's-government now offers health care. Where marriage was once recognized as institution under God, it is now controlled by Man's-government. These are some examples that represent the battle between God's-government and Man's-government. There has been a literal shift from governing ourselves under God to being governed under the rule of Man. Mankind, in our ambition and arrogance, has been battling God for His position since the beginning of time, vying for the spot of "Ruler of Men." Whose side have you been on? Are you sure?

What is Man's-government?

Before going any further, we must distinguish the difference between politics and Man's-government, as they are not one in the same. When most people speak of Government, they are actually referring more to politics, rather than the actual concept of government, which is found throughout nature. Once fully understood, Government can be your best friend or your worst enemy. It can offer you freedom or enslave you for life. It can empower you or defeat you. So, it is very important to understand it, respect it and use it accordingly.

Politics: the ideological belief/discussion of what someone believes the solution may be to a particular problem. When people discuss politics, they are generally discussing what they believe needs to happen in order to solve a particular problem or challenge. Although discussions can become heated at times, there is nothing inherently wrong with political discussions/debates and they should be encouraged. Also, considering it is the nature of Man to ignore those solutions that God has already provided to us, we can pretty much guarantee that we will always have political discussions.

Man's-government (a.k.a Government): the "forced" implementation of political ideas. Government implements political policy via various laws, regulations, mandates and often overreaching executive orders. To ensure that citizens comply with such laws and regulations, Man's-Government utilizes some form of force (sometimes deadly force).

Two types of government

When it comes to the concept of government (to steer), there are two types - God's-government and Man's-government:

God's-government: the free-will implementation of various God-given commandments, morality, virtues and principles found throughout His universe to govern yourself (behave yourself), your relationship with others, your personal affairs and mankind in general. Basically, God's-government is how God would want you to address or solve something (using His methods). God's-government is considered an "internal" form of government, as it operates "within" your conscience mind.

Man's-government: the "forced" implementation of "man-made" ideas and methods to govern over others or to address a particular problem. Man's-government is considered an "external" form of government, since it operates "outside" of your conscience mind. Man's-government either shows up when someone's conscience mind has been breached and they can not behave themselves, or in those situations in society where God's-government has either temporarily failed or expected to. Basically, Man's-government is how "Man" would address a problem if he or she decided against utilizing God's-government.

Based on these two types of government, every political party that exists can be identified or defined by the various amounts of God's-government and Man's-government they use. For example, some political parties utilize more of God's-government in their policies, while other parties seek to increase the role of Man's-government as a necessity towards a particular solution. A quick read of their respective websites will give you an indication of how much of God's-government and Man's-government influence their policies. Hint - the more Government the political party seeks in order to be successful in their goals, the more they fall under Man's-government. However, solutions are found when we operate under the freedom of God's-government, rather than under the force of Man's-government. Political policy should be initially based upon eternal, never-changing principles found within God's nature or universe. For example, one of those principles state that scarcity is created by a rapid increase in demand coupled with a rapid decrease in supply. This "law of nature" represents a universal principle that never changes. However, "human nature" states that human beings will always seek ways of trying to change or challenge that eternal principle. This is because mankind is full of arrogance, which has and will always be the case. This is the same conflict found within God's-government verses Man's-government. The arrogance of Man will always ensure that we will attempt to seek solutions within society using a man-instituted form of government over a God-instituted form of government. This is the very battle that is being waged. The key to finding solutions is to utilize God's-government, as the ways of God will never fail us.

God's-government (internal) and Man's-government (external) are complete opposites of each other and are on sliding scales. When one increases, the other decreases. Therefore, the more you can internally govern yourself under the ways of God, the less you will have to be externally governed by Man. This is evident within the prison system. Because those within the prison system could no longer be trusted to govern themselves appropriately within society, they have been physically removed and governed by the State (Man's-government). Their actions have completely breached God's-government of conscience, morality, virtues, commandments, principles. Therefore, they must be addressed with the force of Man. To keep the inmate's conscience in "check," the prison system utilizes such things as fear and force to govern. However, with force comes enslavement. Thus, because there is an extreme amount of Man's-government within the prison system, an extreme amount of enslavement is also present.

Because God's-government and Man's-government are on sliding scales, anytime you see an increased presence of Man's-government (i.e. the police, the military, entitlement programs or additional laws or regulations), it is an indication that God's-government has broken down, completely failed or is expected to. An increased presence of Man's-government should not be praised or celebrated. It should be viewed as a very sad occasion that the ways of God are no longer present. In other words, the sight of a strong police presence in a community should be a warning sign that those within the community cannot be trusted to govern themselves under the ways of God or it could be that the community has attracted outsiders who cannot govern themselves like-wise. However, Man's-government should be "reactionary," only sought as a "temporary" form of government "after" people have shown that they cannot govern themselves under God's-government. Man's-government should never be a proactive and permanent alternative to God's-government. This is why Christians can't be Democrats. The policies of the Democrat Party seek to pro-actively expand Man's-government as a necessity to advance some of its goals (i.e. equality, fairness and job/financial security). However, when you usher in Man's-government as a proactive alternative to God's-government, it implies that either you never had faith or have lost faith in God's way being the long-term solution to our social ills.

Now that you have a general understanding of the battle between God's-government and Man's-government, how do you know if you are casting your political vote for God or Man? How do you ensure that you are casting an edu-cated vote for those political candidates who seek to govern (steer) over you if you do not know how to qualify them for the position? It is not enough to just listen to their rhetoric on their various political plans. Such talk only serves as smoke and mirrors - keeping you confused until it is time to vote. To better qualify them for the position, you must first understand the role that they will play, once elected. To qualify them for the position, you must first understand what the general concept of government is and is not. Have you ever wondered why so many politicians have so many different viewpoints on how they would govern over you? It is because each are starting from different "political" refer-ence points. The reason many politicians and political parties are so divided is that while they may know plenty about politics, they know very little about the concept of government. In other words, they may know plenty about human nature, but little about God's governing principles found within nature. Their political self-interest is based on their role as a politician (i.e. self) before the principles of good government, which would benefit the People most. Many are so self-absorbed in being our leader, provider, problem solver and "savior" that their arrogance will not allow them to realize that we already have a leader, a problem solver, a provider and a "Savior" - God. However, what would happen if most of them started at the same reference point? What if they started from the same reference point of the concept of "government" rather than "politics?" There would be a better chance of their political talking points being strikingly similar than dissimilar and/or divisive. We would certainly experience more unity than discourse. This is because government is the underlying foundation for politics.

What is the role of Man's-government?

The role of Man's-government is stated within our Declaration of Independence:

"We hold these truths to be self-evident, that all men are created equal, that they are endowed by their Creator with certain unalienable rights, that among these are life, liberty and the pursuit of happiness. That to secure these rights, governments are instituted among men, deriving their just powers from the consent of the governed."

The first line states that all people are "created" as equals under God and that He has endowed each of us with Rights, which are unalienable (nontransferable). The second line states that Government is a "man-made" institution, created to protect the unalienable Rights that God has given to all individuals and to accomplish this, Government must be "just" (morally upright) in its authority and also have the consent of the governed (the People).

Per the Declaration of Independence, the litmus test for a legitimate form of Man's-government is:

- it must protect Rights (which come from God)

- it must be just (morally upright) in its actions

- it must have the consent of the People it will govern over

If all three items are not met, then Government has breached its authority and duties to the People.

It is important to note that the Declaration states that "governments are instituted among men." In other words, God did not create the institution of Man's-government - it is "man-made." God already laid His foundation for the type of government that we are supposed to govern ourselves under - His government. This is crucial to understanding why Christians can't be Democrats. This is because Man's-government and God's-government are opposites of each other! God's-government is what we are supposed to model our lives and decisions after - Man's-government is what we get when we refuse or fail to do so. When we seek Man's way, understand that God's way is pushed out. Christians should not be supporting a political party that openly calls for more of Man's-government as a solution to our problems as this is opposite of God's-government. God commands us to use His. This is because when you invite man-made institutions to the solution table, you get man-made solutions, rather than God-instituted solutions. Government was not created to provide solutions. Solutions are found within the God-endowed talents, gifts and ambitions of the People.

To reiterate, the "primary" role of Man's-government is to protect "every" individual's God-given Rights. In other words, Government is supposed to use its "force" to protect the Rights endowed by God- the "Source." The Force protects the Source. Nowhere in the Declaration does it state that Man's-government's role is to become a secondary "Source" of endowments. There is only one "Source," which is God. When Man's-government attempts to become another "source," it only comes in as competition with God. Now, regarding God-given Rights, it does not matter the age, gender, ethnicity, sexual preference, economic status or any other attribute of the individual. It is the role of Government to protect their Rights above all else. The exception to that rule is when that individual decides to infringe upon the Rights of others. At that point, all bets are off. However, for Government to effectively protect our unalienable Rights from God, the concept of Rights must first be defined. (This will be explained in detail in chapter 3 - That's my Right, right?). For now, a "Right" can be simply defined as any act that does not require permission from another person. For example, you do not have to ask permission of anyone to lift your left leg. Therefore, lifting your left leg is your God-given Right. In regards to politicians, their responsibility is to "protect" God-given Rights, not "replace" them nor define what they are. Notice that the Declaration nor the Constitution state that the role of Government is to help your buy your first home, fund your college education, pay your mortgage, feed you, loan money to your business or help you or your neighbor down the street. This is because none of these things are God-given Rights or legitimate functions of the Government. Each time the Government enacts such entitlements, it is always at the loss of someone else's Rights. Anytime Government removes or denies you use of your God-given Right, it has failed in its duty. Again, the exception is if someone uses their Right(s) to deny you the use of yours. When this happens, it is the duty of Government to intervene.

The Declaration of Independence is a crucial element to our freedom. It gives us the formula for how independence works, establishes a belief in a Creator, defines where Rights come from and determines the role of Man's-government. However, since it is rarely discussed nor being taught from these perspectives, our God-given Rights and liberties have diminished over time and are at risk of being completely lost.

Why do we need Government?

We need government for one, simple fact - humans are imperfect beings. Not only are we imperfect, we are also social beings. We have an innate requirement for social interaction with other human beings. We live and thrive in various social orders and communities with other imperfect humans. However, because of our imperfections, we are unable to govern (behave) ourselves appropriately for every minute of every hour of every day of every year. So, during those times when our conscience becomes low and our level of morality becomes questionable, some type of external force is required to ensure that we do not completely misbehave and possibly infringe upon the God-given Rights of others. Man's-government is this "external force" that keeps us in "check." It uses force to act as an "equalizer," showing up in those places where your sense of God's-government has failed. Basically, the less you can govern (behave) yourself, the more Man's-government is needed to force you to. For instance, when a child becomes angry and unable to self-govern (behave themselves), the parent (a form of Man's-government) uses some type of force to correct the child's behavior. Because of the potential damage that unruly behavior can cause to others and/or property, Man's-government must always show up with more force than the threat itself. In other words, the greater the threat, the greater the force needed to deal with it. This is true within the home, within communities, within all aspects of nature and throughout the world. This greater amount of force allows the potential threat to be quickly controlled. Whenever Rights are threatened, Man's-government is supposed to use its authority and force to reestablish order as quick as possible. It serves as a protective shield, fencing us off from each other whenever needed. This is shown in picture #1.

Picture #1

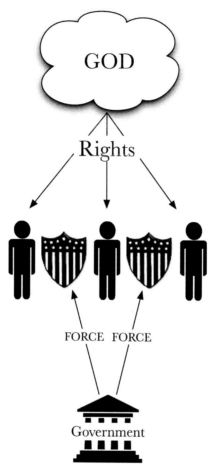

Government was created to use its force as a
way to shield us from each other, so that we do
not infringe upon another's God-given Rights.

"If men were angels, no government would be necessary"
~ James Madison

Government exists to protect us from each other. Where
government has gone beyond its limits is in deciding
to protect us from ourselves. ~ Ronald Reagan

Practical examples of government

As previously stated, the concept of government goes beyond politically-related government that most of us are familiar with. Government can be found in every aspect of our lives. For example, every time you are driving on the road, you encounter various "internal" and "external" forms of government. Some of the internal forms of government are courtesy, consideration and patience. Again, these virtues (high moral standards) reside in your inner-conscience. Some of the external types include stop signs, traffic lights, speed bumps and speed limit signs, etc. These serve to govern (steer) your conscience while driving. You are also governed by the painted lines in the road that ensure that you stay in your lane. Every now and then, both the internal and external types of government break down. For instance, drivers know that when a traffic signal has malfunctioned, they are supposed to treat the intersection as a four-way stop. However, we have all experienced situations where this rule was ignored (always the other driver, of course). Now, depending on the importance of the intersection, the malfunctioning traffic signal may be replaced by another form of external government, such as a traffic officer. Again, like the previous form of external government (the traffic signal), the officer is not really directing traffic - they are actually directing "conscience." The officer represents a physical force that governs (steer) the conscience of those drivers who cannot be expected to internally govern themselves under the virtues of courtesy, consideration and patience.

Another real-world example of government would be a bouncer in a night-club. When patrons are unable to govern themselves, due to a low conscience and a drop in morality, they are "externally" governed by the bouncer (often using physical force). Just like Man's-government, the bouncer must put down the potential threat as quickly as possible. This is for the safety of the other patrons and property. The bouncers are normally physically threatening in size and strength. This acts as a deterrent, which is no different from how our military and police "force" operate. Both the bouncer and Government utilize the force of Man's-government to keep order.

Sometimes we purposely use various forms of external government upon ourselves, especially in those situations where we realize that we cannot govern ourselves under the ways of God. We may physically fence ourselves off from access to certain foods, addictive habits and even other people. At other times, we seek the assistance of others to externally govern us. For example, those who may conclude that they are not financially thrift could allow someone else to manage their financial affairs, fencing themselves off from their funds. It is because we are imperfect that various external forms of government are required in our society. However, the caveat is that the more external government we have, the more enslaved we become to its force.

Man's-government (master or servant?)

Is Government the master or servant of its citizens?

"De-legate" - to entrust (a task or responsibility) to another person, typically one who is less senior than oneself

"De" - Down or Away (origin Latin)

The prefix "de" means down or away. There are many words in the English language prefixed with "de" that imply such (i.e. debase, defend, defeat and demean). In regards to the hierarchy between the People (us) and Government, an appropriate word would be "delegation." When you delegate a task to someone, it is often to someone who is beneath you in a particular hierarchy. We, the People, are supposed to delegate to those in Government. This implies that Government is inferior to the People. In addition, per the Declaration of Independence, Government gets its authority and power from the consent of the governed (the People). Thus, initial authority and power are held in the hands of the People; Government has no true power of its own. It only has the power and resources that we allow it to have. Whenever you consent your authority to someone, along with your financial resources, it is with the implied understanding that they serve you - not that you serve them. This being the case, Government would fall into the category of a servant of the People - not master. However, once the People allow Government officials to start believing that they are no longer servants of the People, but their masters, tyranny (cruel and oppressive rule) starts to creep in. This is a natural power progression and the current state in which our Government operates - as our superiors, delegating to us. Since 1776, we have gone from a nation in which Government serves us, to a nation where we serve Government.

Picture #2 reflects the original model in which Government was to operate. We, the People, were to serve and be accountable to God and Man's-government was to serve and be accountable to the People.

Original Declaration Model:

- God endowed each individual with Rights

- The People formed a social compact (US Constitution) with the Government, restraining its authority and reach

- Government's role was to protect our unalienable (non-transferable) Rights from God.

- The Government is accountable to the People.

- We, the People, are accountable to God.

Original Declaration Model

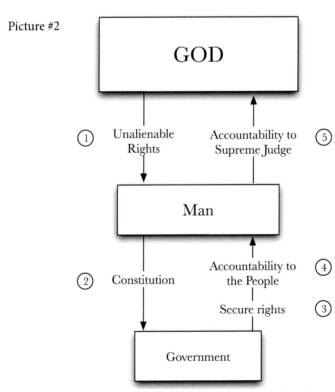

Picture #2

(Image used by permission of Joseph Andrews)

Picture #3 represents where we are today. Notice that God is no longer relevant, as his provisions and endowments are now being provided by Man's-government. Where Government used to be accountable to the People, the People are now accountable to Government. No longer are the People nor Man's-government accountable to God - He is now absent.

Current Model

Picture #3

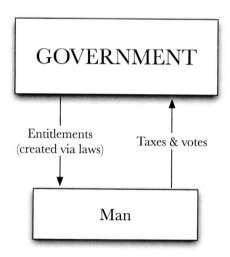

(*Image used by permission of Joseph Andrews*)

One of the main reasons why Christians can't be Democrats is because the Democrat Party believes in providing for the needs of its citizens, which only further expands and perpetuates this current-day Declaration model. Thus, the People will always remain inferior to Government, enslaved by dependency and the heavy tax burden needed to support the entitlements. As voting Christians, we should be reestablishing the hierarchy of God being our provider (original Declaration model), not supporting the expansion of the current-day model.

God's-basket

God is the source of all things that are good (this would be a good time to confirm this statement on your list/bookmark). When we are born, God endows each of us with our own "God-basket." Your basket is filled with His goodness. It contains everything necessary for you to chart your destiny and live your life to fulfill God's purpose. The items within your basket allow you to govern (steer) your own ship. One of the worst things you can do is lose those items within your basket. This will prove to be a great disservice to yourself, to your loved ones and to God. In other words, when God gives you something, you can bet that it is in your best interest to you protect and keep it. Yet, when you purposely discard these items from your basket or worse, when you give consent for Man's-government to remove them, you lose the "goodness" that God has personally given to you. Without these things in your basket, you will become lost, weak, and ultimately powerless. Until you go out and retrieve them or replace them, you will certainly lose your way. Therefore, keep a firm grip on your God-basket. Also, be forewarned that Government has its own basket, however, it is "not" from God - it is man-made. It contains such things as force, fear, dependency, debt and other vices (immoral things). So, watch out for the old Government "switcheroo" trick. Let us take a look at what is in your God-basket (Picture #4).

Picture #4

God and Government's Baskets

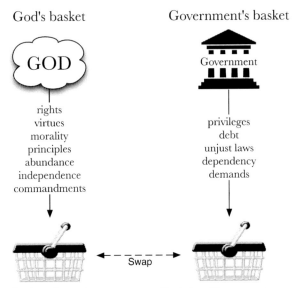

God's basket

Government's basket

GOD

Government

rights
virtues
morality
principles
abundance
independence
commandments

privileges
debt
unjust laws
dependency
demands

Swap

Each of us have been given a God basket, which is filled with the very things we need to steer our own lives

Each time Government swaps out what's in God's basket for something in its basket, all of society suffers

Each time Government replaces a Right with a privilege, a command with a demand & principles with unjust laws, God's basket slowly transforms into Government's basket

18

The things in your God-basket represent "power." So, be on guard, as those things that become void of power eventually stop moving or die. When Government sucks enough of God's power from the People, society collapses and dies. This has been the cycle of all civilizations that have come and gone. Those things inside your basket are on loan to you from God. Thus, your power from God is on loan too. To retain your power from God, it is important that you defend every item in your basket. There will be plenty of people and politicians who seek to increase their own basket by enticing you to hand over what is in yours - mainly your Rights. When they cannot entice you with their trickery, they will attempt to outright steal them from you by resorting to legislative measures or physical force. The best way to protect what is in your basket is to prevent Man's-government from ever putting its hands in it. The main purpose of the Constitution is to restrain Man's-government from doing just that. "Whose basket are you currently operating out of?"

Takeaways:

- God's-government (freedom) and Man's-government (force) are opposites of each other.

- Inviting Government into your life is the equivalent of inviting force.

- Government's role is to protect your God-given Rights (located in your God-basket) - not decide what your Rights are.

- The Force is supposed to protect the Source, not be in competition with God.

- Government is accountable to the People and we are accountable to God.

Man's-government is not love, abundance, morality or freedom - it is force! This cannot be stressed enough. The authority to use force to accomplish its goals is what separates Government from all other man-made institutions. Both you and Government cannot be responsible for any given decision in your life. Unfortunately, our nation is moving back under Government rule and away from God's rule. We have foolishly sat idle and allowed Government to be the keeper of God's Rights. Along the way, we have empowered Man's-government with those very same things we could have done ourselves. Each time we empower Government with a new responsibility, the cost is our power and money and increased force.

> "A wise and frugal Government, which shall restrain men from injuring one another, which shall leave them otherwise free to regulate their own pursuits of industry and improvement, and shall not take from the mouth of labor the bread it has earned. This is the sum of good government, and this is necessary to close the circles of our felicities." ~ Thomas Jefferson

Question - As a Christian, how can you chart and "steer" a course to serve and fulfill God's purpose in your life if someone else is doing the driving?

CHAPTER 3

THAT'S MY RIGHT, RIGHT?

"A nation of well informed men who have been taught to know and prize the rights which God has given them cannot be enslaved. It is in the region of ignorance that tyranny begins."
~ *Benjamin Franklin*

"In Republics, the great danger is, that the majority may not sufficiently respect the rights of the minority."
~ *James Madison*

We hear a lot about "Rights." There are human rights, civil rights, gay rights, minority rights, women rights, healthcare rights, workers rights, voting rights, earth rights, animal rights and the list goes on for what seems like forever. There appears to be a Right for any and everything. There seems to be a new segment of the population demanding a new "Right" for someone or something almost monthly. Why do so many people feel that their particular Rights are being infringed upon and/or denied? It is mostly likely because the common understanding of what constitutes a Right has slowly eroded over the past two hundred or so years. Many people insist that they have a "Constitutional" Right of "blah, blah, blah." Any mention of "Constitutional Rights" by someone probably is an indication that they are not aware of what defines a Right or where they come from. Case in point - I have the Right to twitch my nose, yet that Right is not listed anywhere within the US Constitution. Considering that it is not there, do I now lose my Right to twitch my nose? Hardly! This is because your Rights do not come from the Constitution. As previous stated, the Constitution was written with the purpose of constraining and limiting the power and reach of the Federal Government. Over time, the Constitution has morphed into some sort of elevated "Super document." This is the very reason we have so much political contention. Too many people are looking towards the Constitution to provide the very answers that it was not written to provide. So, if Rights do not come from the Constitution, then where do they come from? Well, if you didn't catch the answer while reading chapter 2, the answer can also be found by referring back to the Declaration of Independence.

The Origin of Rights

The second paragraph of the Declaration of Independence begins:

"We hold these truths to be self-evident, that all men are created equal, that they are endowed by their Creator with certain unalienable rights ...."

Eureka! Yep, that's right! Rights come from God! God has endowed each of us with Rights. Not only that, when we are created, we each get exactly the same Rights as those people created before and after us. The Declaration states that God has endowed us with "Rights." Notice that the word "Rights" is not pre-fixed with a subcategorized term. That is because God does not endow us with subdivided or hyphenated rights. Rights are defined by their origin of source (God), not by how they are morally or immorally applied by someone. The concept of "hyphenated Rights" was a man-made creation - not God-created. Their purpose is to attract attention to what some believe is an unfair situation or a flat out denial of their Rights. However, after applying the litmus test for Rights and privileges (later in this chapter), you will be surprised to learn that the "Rights" most groups protest for are actually privileges being masqueraded as Rights. When you convert privileges into Rights, it weakens the validity and the differences between the two. Due to its political correctness, the potential damage of the "hyphenated" Right is that it perpetuates segregation within society. People subdivide themselves into segregated groups, each making demands of the Government to advance their specific cause. In regards to the stated duty of Man's-government, there should be no recognition of the "hyphenated" Rights. They are simply "Rights!"

How do we know that Rights come from God? Barring a very deep philosophical explanation, a very simple way of knowing that Rights do not come from Man is to acknowledge what we already know about mankind. We are emotional, volatile, unpredictable and inconsistent creatures. Our minds and moods change with the wind. Rights, on the other hand, require eternal consistency, which is only found within God. If Rights came from Man, they would be in a constant state of flux. With each election cycle and change of Government, Rights would most likely have to be redefined. What was considered a Right one year might not be the next. For something to qualify as a Right, its implied ownership must be eternal and consistent (i.e. minute-to-minute, hour-to-hour, day-to-day and year-to-year). You cannot have a consistent and persistent Right based on inconsistent shifting whims of Man.

Because God is infinite, so are our Rights in nature. They cannot all be listed within any document or contained within a computer database. There is an infinite amount of things you can do that qualifies as a Right (not requiring the permission from others). The Declaration of Independence lists the most recognized Rights of "life, liberty and the pursuit of happiness." However, the whole sentence reads:

> "We hold these truths to be self-evident, that all men are created equal, that they are endowed by their Creator with certain unalienable rights, that among these are life, liberty and the pursuit of happiness."

Notice the words, "that *among* these are ..." The word "among" is key! It implies that there are more God-given Rights than just "life, liberty and the pursuit of happiness." Although there are some additional Rights listed within the US Constitution, it is *not* the source document for determining what all of our Rights are. As a matter of fact, if all of our God-given Rights were to be listed within the US Constitution, someone would still be writing it! Now considering that all of our Rights cannot possibly be listed, the following litmus test can be used to identify a Right:

Rights:

- are endowed (given) by the Creator/God

- they do not require permission from others (since they come from God)

- are unalienable (non-transferable)

As mentioned, Rights are defined by the source from which they came - God. They are "not" defined by being morally "right or wrong" in their usage or by your age, ethnic background, sexual preference, financial status, etc. For example, feeding someone in need may be the "right" thing to do, but that noble thought does not grant you an elevated Right or authority to break into a grocery store to accomplish the task. Not only would this be breaking God's law (i.e. stealing), but recall that Government's role is to intervene, in order to stop you from infringing upon the property Rights of the store owner. Therefore, you would also be breaking Government's law. Also, because Government is supposed to protect our property Rights, it would also be wrong to use Man's-Government to perform the same noble deed. Considering that Government has no resources of its own, the very moment that you utilize it as a means to provide for others, God's commandment not to steal must also be broken. You can not break one commandment to fulfill another. Now, using the example of helping someone in need, let's analyze what really happens when we utilize Man's-government to do the will of God.

Under Man's-government:

- In the name of human compassion, the Government uses its force to "legally" confiscate the property from one segment of the population (Group A) to feed another (Group B). However, because force was used, the very compassion that served as motivation is now completely absent from the act (this is because force is not an attribute of compassion).

- The role of Government changes - Government's role goes from "protecting" everyone's property Rights to confiscating property and "providing" it to others. Property rights of "Group A" are lost in an effort to provide a privilege for "Group B." (to seek help is a Right; to be helped by others is a privilege).

- The scales of God's-government and Man's-government tilts towards Man - the power and authority of Man's-government increases and the concept of God-given Rights for the individual decreases.

- Both groups become enslaved - "Group A" become chattel (forced) slaves to Government - They are now legally enslaved under laws that permit the legal confiscation of their property at the benefit of other group. "Group B" becomes indentured (enticed) slaves under Government - to ensure that such laws that benefit them remain in existence, "Group B" must always stay in the good graces of Government, thus guaranteeing a vote (i.e. power) for the politician.

Now, let's compare this to how someone should be helped under the methods of God's-government:

- In the name of love and human compassion, individuals willingly share their own blessings to help those in "Group B." Since force was *not* used, love and compassion remain present during the act of giving.

- The role of Government remains neutral, as it is not involved in the process. Individual property is protected. Legalized Government robbery is averted.

- The scale of God's-government and Man's-government shifts towards God - Individual Rights are preserved and God's commands are followed.

- Both "Group A" and "Group B" remain free people during the process. The authority of the politician is decreased or kept in check.

Although the person was eventually helped in both scenarios, using Government to perform the deed required breaking God's commandments, enslaved both groups and increased the power of Man's-government. When comparing these two scenarios, understand that everyone will not participate under God's way. When people are offered the choice to voluntarily participate in something, many will not. This is okay - it is their Right not to. You will never get 100% participation. As a possible comfort, recall that God does not have 100% of people believing in Him and He created us! In other words, if you set your expectations higher than God's, you will surely be disappointed.

"Duty is ours; results are God's" ~ *John Quincy Adams*

Who owns your Rights?

The Declaration of Independence states that God has created each of us and endowed each of us with Rights. Well, if God endowed you with Rights, then you own them! You can choose to exercise them and/or refuse to exercise them at will. However, if Government denies you usage of your Rights and/or forces you to exercise them, then they were not really your Rights to begin with, were they? This is the danger of Man's-government and no political party has a complete monopoly on this position. On a political left-right spectrum, political groups on the right tend to deny Rights, while those parties on the left tend to remove Rights altogether. Although both positions are wrong, a denial of Rights at least implies that the political party recognizes that you have the Right, but simply denies you access to it. This is far better than those political parties that remove Rights, implying that you never had the Right to begin with. In other words, it is better to be denied access to something than to be told that it never existed. Either way, there is nothing within the Declaration of Independence that implies that God endowed Man's-government to manage our Rights or to redistribute them later at their leisure. Since Government is not the giver of Rights, it should not be in the business of managing them. Its intervention should only come into play when two or more Rights are in conflict of each other. Yet, there are many unjust Government laws that deny or remove the Rights that God has given us, all in the name of "good intentions," of course. The very fact that we have to petition Government for the usage of certain Rights should be an indication that Government has grown beyond its initial role and power. It is important that we restore the Rights God have given us. Be wary of anyone who campaigns on removing them from you and/or others.

God, who is the source of freedom and independence, gives us the free will to use our Rights in the manner that we choose. Obviously, it is best that we utilize our Rights in responsible, considerate, respectful and compassionate ways. Unfortunately, some people will chose to exercise their God-given Rights in immoral ways, yet it is still their Right to do so. When this happens, we must refrain from using the institution of Government as a way to "fix" their immorality. Recall, Government is the protector of Rights, not the moral authority over them. Thus, it is not the role of Government nor any individual to determine under what circumstances anyone should utilize their Rights. "You" own you and "you" own your Rights. You, nor your Rights, are property of the Government or others.

Rights are deteriorating

As society, in general, moves away from its belief in God, the premise of where Rights come from start to deteriorate. In other words, Rights can not come from the Creator if we no longer believe that a Creator exists. If we no longer believe, as a society, in a power that is higher than Man, then how will we differentiate between Rights and privileges? What would be the litmus test for both? As a whole, previous generations believed that Rights came from God. However, if we continue down the current path of allowing Government to remove God and references of God from our society, so goes the source of Rights. Without God, there can not be any rights, only Government privileges. The moment Rights are defined as coming from Mankind or Government, they become alienable (transferable).

Privileges come from Man

If Rights come from God, then privileges come from Man or Government. They are identified by the following litmus test:

Privileges:

- require permission from others or Government

- are granted or earned by/from others or Government

- are alienable (transferable and temporarily granted)

- come with a tangible (physical) or implied license of usage

The general rule is if you have to ask permission before doing something, then it is a privilege. When someone extends a privilege to you, it comes with a license of usage. The license may be tangible (which you can physically touch), like drivers license, or implied, such as eating at a restaurant. The restaurant does not extend a tangible license to everyone who enters. The process would take too long and most likely discourage patrons. It is implied that the restaurant owner is extending the privilege to those entering. Because those working within the restaurant cannot force you to dine there, you are also extending them the privilege of serving you.

Privileges are alienable (transferable). This means that privileges can be transferred, granted or revoked at any time. Using the example of the restaurant, once you leave the establishment, the two-way privilege between the patron and business owner is revoked. At the moment you return to dine at a future date, the privilege is temporarily granted again. However, if it has been decided that you are no longer welcomed in the restaurant, your license of usage for future visits is permanently revoked. In the case of some businesses, tangible licenses are issued (i.e. a visitor's badge). The badge is an indication that you have permission to be on the premises. When you leave the property, the badge is returned, thus your privilege has expired for that particular visit.

Considering that Rights come from God and privileges come from Man and Government, every time you support Government's removal of an individual's Right in lieu of a privilege, you are advocating removing something out of someone's God basket, while helping to increase the authority of Man's-Government. You are literally denying what God has given and replacing it with what Man is allowing.

It makes no difference if you morally agree/disagree with how someone is utilizing their Rights. They may be exercising their Right to be greedy. Although you may morally disagree with Man's greed (a vice), it is still their God-given Right to be greedy. God does not condone greed, but He allows it because of His unconditional love for us (love = freedom). However, when you authorize Government to use its force to address that greed, the "Right" to be greedy is lost and greed becomes a Government privilege. Sooner than later, everything considered immoral will become a privilege and Rights will cease to exist.

The Hierarchical order of Rights and Privileges

The reason why we still struggle in our efforts to improve society is because we continue to replace the methods of God with the ways of Man. When you allow Government privileges to trump God-given Rights, you effectively aid Man's-government in its battle against God's-government. If you truly believe that God is the "solution," then you must resist the temptation to give Government the authority to replace Rights with privileges. Man's-government will continue to push for more of your power under the premise of "doing what is best" for society. The more Government becomes a substitution for God, the more God's presence is eradicated out of society. This is because you cannot serve two masters - God and Government. The love of God and the force of

28

Man cannot occupy the same space and time anywhere in God's universe. Each time you authorize Government to remove someone's Rights in lieu of providing privileges to others, you are aiding in destroying the hierarchy order of God over Government (picture #5). As Christians, it is important that we protect what God has given, even if we disagree with how it is being generally applied. The best way to address someone you consider morally "irresponsible" with their Rights is to encourage them to seek God and His love. Let *Him* handle it. Do not be too quick to invite Government. It always enters with force, fear and dependency. It *never* utilizes God's love.

Picture #5

Rights and Privileges Hierarchy

1. God is above Man, therefore God-given Rights should be above & take priority over Government/Man-privileges.

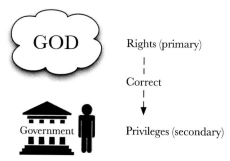

2. However, when Government/Man privileges take priority over God-given Rights, the hierarchy is reversed & dysfunction occurs within society.

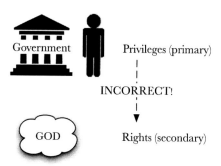

The role of Man's-government is to protect God-given Rights before protecting privileges. This ensures that the integrity of the hierarchy remains intact.

Is it a Right or a Privilege?

Apply the Rights/Privileges litmus test to determine if the following examples fall under a Right or a privilege:

Rights:

- are endowed (given) by the Creator/God

- they do not require permission from others (since they come from God)

- are unalienable (non-transferable)

Privileges:

- require permission from others or Government

- are granted or earned by/from others or Government

- are alienable (transferable and temporarily granted)

- come with a tangible (physical) or implied license of usage

Marriage?
Marriage is not a Right - it is a privilege. You only have the Right to pursue a potential spouse for marriage. Although God instituted marriage, it is considered a two-way privilege, as requires the consent of both people. However, now that Government has usurped (taken without authority) God's institution of marriage, you are also required to get its permission too, which comes complete with a tangible marriage "license." Speaking of, why is any political party involved in God's institution of marriage? Who is Man to take what God has given?

Education?
You only have a Right to seek an education or to educate yourself, but you do not have a God-given Right/entitlement to be educated by others. You are not entitled to someone educating you. That is their choice

to do so. Out of Government's own lack of understanding between Rights and privileges, it has erroneously deemed education a Right and therefore has given itself the justification to tax its citizens to obtain the resources to fund what really is a privilege. The Government has even gotten into the business of providing student loans. Where in the Constitution does the Federal government have the authority to do so? It does not. Government has extended its authority beyond the Constitution simply by convincing enough of us that certain privileges should actually be Rights (BTW - isn't conversion illegal?). Its citizens, who are supposed to be the guardians of the Constitution, cannot validate this claim, because the difference between Rights and privileges are no longer generally understood.

Killing?
Contrary to belief and as harsh as it may sound, killing is actually a Right, not a privilege, as no prior permission is required from Man. However, keep in mind that we were commanded by God not to murder. Also, recall that Man's-government was instituted to protect an individual's Right to life and therefore must intercede and prevent the act. This is a legitimate purpose of Government. In terms of hunting, Government has converted this Right to kill into a privilege. This is confirmed by the fact that you must get prior permission from Government to hunt. If permission is granted, you are issued a tangible hunting license, which can be revoked at any time.

Some examples of various Rights and privileges:

- Entering someone's home/business is a privilege. You temporary suspend certain Rights in exchange for having the privilege of entering.

- Raising your left arm is a Right.

- Living an unhealthy lifestyle is your Right.

- Seeking food is a Right; being fed by others is a privilege.

- Hate is wrong, but is a God-given Right. No person extends another the privilege of hating them.

- Healthcare is a privilege, not a Right. You have no God-given Right to demand that someone else to be responsible for your health.

- Joining the military is not a Right - it is a privilege. You cannot just show up and enlist yourself.

- No one has a Right to a job. Performing a job for someone is a two-way privilege, as both employer and employee must give prior consent. However, both have the Right to terminate the relationship.

- There is no God-given Right to equality or fairness. Life is not fair and no amount of Government intervention can fix that. However, we should be fair, equal and just to each other out of being morally upright.

It is important to remember that just because something is your God-given Right does not mean it will not come with consequences if exercised in an immoral manner. So be sure to play nice. Be responsible with what God has given you, even when others are not. Be sure to obey and respect structure and rules. Accepting rules is an acknowledgment that you will "obey to play." It implies that you are willing to keep your Rights in check, in order to participate in the privilege offered to you.

Takeaways:

- Rights come from God; privileges come from Government or Man.

- Rights do not require permission; privileges do. They are opposites of each other.

- Government's primary role is to protect Rights, not dictate them.

- Rights do not come from the Constitution; they come from God.

- There are no hyphenated Rights - they are just "Rights."

- Each person has the same number of Rights - no more, no less.

Our system of Government in the United States is predicated on the premise of God-given rights. However, if Government will not protect our Rights, then why would we expect it to protect any of our other blessings or endowments from God? Without this protection, anything and everything will be up for grabs. The very same Government that was given the responsibility to protect these Rights is the same Government that is now robbing us of them. This is equivalent to hiring someone to protect your home, only to later find out that they are robbing it!

The reason why Christians can't be Democrats is because the stated policies of the Democrat Party call for a direct push for Government-forced equality, fairness and security (in terms of entitlements). Although these are noble ideas, forcing them requires that the authority of Man's-government be increased (thus decreasing God's-government). Such policies must also rob someone else of their God-given Rights in the process. This is accomplished either by laws or through the confiscation of their personal property via taxes. Government-forced equality, fairness and entitlements cannot be successfully accomplished for certain groups without removing the Rights of another's. This is a natural principle found throughout God's universe. Forced equality, fairness or provisions is not a method that Christ would use or condone - nor should we. Not only that, the governed (the People) cannot give Government the authority to do something that they, themselves, can not legally do. When we allow Man's-government to snatch away the Rights that God has given to others, by no means are we moving towards God - we are literally moving in the opposite direction.

CHAPTER 4

ALL MEN ARE INDEED CREATED EQUAL

"A society that puts equality ahead of freedom, will end up with neither equality nor freedom." ~ *Milton Friedman*

Most everyone has heard the phrase, "All men are created equal." Various activist groups have used the phrase to imply that there is a God-given Right to equal opportunity, equal access or equal outcome. I consider the phrase one of the most misinterpreted, misused, dangerous and damaging phrases uttered in political debates. It has been used to justify Government-forced equal opportunity, which enslaves all involved and removes personal Rights. This is because forced equality cannot be accomplished without forcing someone to readjust his or her position in the situation. In other words, if you want "equal," someone has to be prevented from advancing while everyone else catches up. For example, if you wanted the outcome of a track and field race to be "equal," you would either be required to slow down the faster runners so the slower runners could catch up or give the slower runners a head start. I call this, "moving at the speed of slow." However, this principle of equality does not operate like this in nature. Therefore, forced equality is a man-made creation, which attempts to manipulate principles in nature - God's nature. In its current "misunderstanding" and usage, "all men are created equal" is the greatest enemy of freedom and liberty. Although commonly mistaken as part of the Constitution, it actually comes from the US Declaration of Independence:

> "We hold these truths to be self-evident, that all men are created equal, that they are endowed by their Creator with certain, unalienable rights, that among these are life, liberty and the pursuit of happiness."

It states "all men are created equal." Yet, each of us has different and varying looks, tastes, beliefs, skills, talents, etc. Some people are born with mental and physical disabilities and others with certain diseases. Some are born into wealth, while others into poverty. It is quite obvious that when we are born, we are not created equal. So, how could we all be created equal, yet be so different? What exactly does the phrase mean? An exploration of the "Divine Right of Kings" will hopefully offer clarity.

The Divine Right of Kings

During a certain time period in history, there was a general belief in the concept of the "Divine Right of Kings." The People believed that God sent kings to rule over them. In other words, kings ruled under the premise of "Divine" authority from God. This belief established the hierarchy of God over the king and the king over the People. (picture #6)

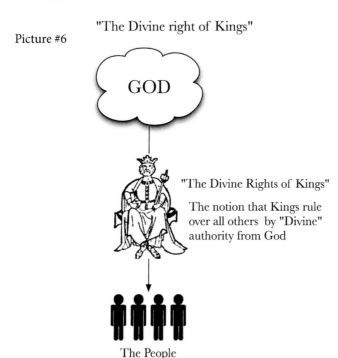

Picture #6

"The Divine right of Kings"

GOD

"The Divine Rights of Kings"

The notion that Kings rule over all others by "Divine" authority from God

The People

Not only did this hierarchy put people in an inferior position to the king, but also created the perfect scenario for kings to abuse their power. Not only that, it made it very difficult to challenge the king's actions or leadership if you believed he was God-sent. King George III, the British king during the American Revolutionary war, did abuse such power, so much so that the "27 abuses of King George III" are listed within our Declaration of Independence. People cannot obtain God's independence if a tyrant King is lodged in-between. Therefore, "the King must go!" The Founders had to dislodge the king from his divine throne, if they were to ever gain the freedom and liberty that only God could offer. The phrase, "all men are created equal" did just that. In other words, "all men are created equal" means absolutely ALL of mankind, including kings, are "created" by God and "equal" under God, with equal amounts of endowed Rights. It does not mean that we all have equal access to certain things, equal treatment by others, equal opportunities or equal results in life. It means that when we are created, we all start off as equals "under" God; that no person was created "above" others in the eyes of God. This strongly implies that God does not send anyone to rule over you. God is the ruler of mankind, not men, be it kings or Government. They are just men. "All men are created equal" effectively placed kings on "equal" footing with all mankind and abolished the concept of the Divine Right of Kings. (See picture #7)

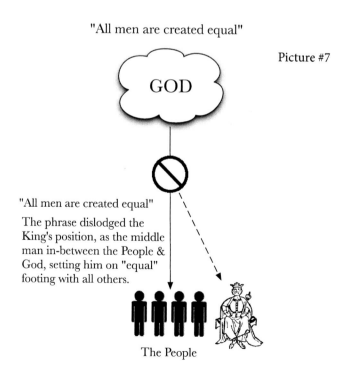

"All men are created equal"

Picture #7

GOD

"All men are created equal"

The phrase dislodged the King's position, as the middle man in-between the People & God, setting him on "equal" footing with all others.

The People

"All men are created equal" both dislodged the King from the position of middleman and reaffirmed the belief that God is the creator of all Mankind. This was all accomplished in five, short words.

The Founders understood the philosophical concept of Government, whether its authority is placed within the hands of Kings or the political "suits" in Washington, DC. It makes no difference if the year is 1776 or 2776, there will always be people who seek more power than God has initially given them. The power they seek is yours!

"The Divine Right of Politicians"

Although no longer officially called the "Divine rights of Kings," many Christians still believe that God has sent certain people within government to rule over them. As before, this creates an inferior mind set and places you in a position of Government servitude. A modern-day term for "The Divine right of Kings" could be, "The Divine Right of Politicians." It is when people believe that politicians are sent by God to rule over them and lead them into the perceived Promised Land. Be assured that there will never be a shortage of those who will happily fill the role and title of "Ruler of Men." Such beliefs somewhat equates the responsibility of the politician to Moses. However, there is a stark difference between Moses and the politician - the Israelites were free to follow Moses under God, but we, the People, are being forcefully dragged behind the politician. Moses led the Israelites away from the Pharaoh (Man's-government), not towards him. The politician utilizes various laws to force us to follow.

Forced equality

For the sake of argument, let us assume that "all men are created equal" actually meant equal access, treatment, opportunity or results. When enforced under Government, an amazing thing happens: everyone eventually becomes enslaved. This is because forced equality and freedom cannot happily coexist anywhere in nature. They both cannot occupy the very same space at the very same time. Equal results and freedom are on sliding scales - as one increases, the other decreases. To better understand how this concept works in God's nature, use a group of people to perform the "133 Crayons experiment." The more people, the better.

133 Crayons group experiment

Items needed:

- One or more boxes of Crayons (the more crayons the better)

- Drawing paper of various colors

- White drawing paper (ensure there is 2 sheets of white paper for each person participating)

- One blue ink pen for each person participating

Preparation:

Separate the paper by color (including the white paper) and place in individual stacks on a table, along with the crayons.

1st drawing exercise:

Instruct the participants to choose any amount of crayons and one sheet of drawing paper (white is permissible). Instruct the participants to take 3-5 minutes to freely draw whatever they want on the paper with their crayons.

2nd drawing exercise:

Pass out one white sheet of paper and one blue ink pen to each participant. Do not let the participants use their own ink pen. All ink pens must be identical. Have each person fold the white sheet of paper vertically, and then unfold it. Now have each person fold the white sheet of paper horizontally, and then unfold it.

If done correctly, there should be a perceived center of the paper where the vertically and horizontal creases meet (the perpendicular). In that perceived center point, have each person make a small dot with the blue ink pen.

Post-instructions:

Instruct everyone to visually share their 1st drawing with the other participants. Notice that no two drawings are alike.

Instruct everyone to visually share their 2nd drawing with the other participants. Notice that all of the drawings are equally the same, a white sheet of paper with a blue ink dot in the perceived middle.

Results:

When you gave everyone the freedom to draw whatever they wanted, you not only got more ideas, the drawings were unequal in both design and perceived talent. This is what freedom gives you - more ideas and innovation, although unequal. In order to ensure "equal" results, you had to remove the freedoms of each individual. The more skilled artists were not able to utilize their God-given talents. They were forcefully limited in their drawing skills to ensure equality.

As you can see, the Founders could not seek independence and freedom while at the same time promoting Government-enforced equality under the premise of "all men are created equal." An eternal principle in God's universe is that freedom creates inequality. Thus, Government-forced equality of any kind removes the freedoms of someone else.

Takeaways:

- God does not send others to rule over you. He is the King and Ruler of mankind.

- We are created as "equals" under God - not Man.

- Forced equality and freedom cannot occupy the same space and time. They are opposites and common foes.

- Freedom creates inequality. Forced equality is the enemy of freedom.

- Equality/fairness are "just" only when done out of personal free will.

Government, when kept within limits, is an effective servant "beneath" the People. However, as it grows, it moves from servant of the People to their ruler and master. It lodges itself in-between the People and God, just like King George III. As Christians, it is important that we do not allow for the expansion of Government's reach and power beyond its primary role of protecting God-given Rights. When we use government to carry out "good intentions" or to force equality, we are only growing its authority. We end up placing those within government in a superior position above us. If you believe that God sent someone to rule over you, then you have already subconsciously placed yourself in an inferior position to him or her. This is no way to live and definitively not a way towards independence. This type of thinking resurrects the concept of the "Divine Right of Kings."

Being created equally under God and treated equally by Man are not one in the same. As a matter of fact, no one has a God-given Right to be treated equally. God wants us to be free, not enslaved under Man's forced and a warped sense of equality and fairness. Once free of Government's forceful grip, we can create equality and fairness by freely sharing our blessings with others, as we are commanded to do. Equality that is morally "just" can only be accomplished by individuals in the private sector (non-government sector of society), using the virtues of God's-government. When equality is forcefully attempted in the public sector (Government), it is unjust and Man's-rule is increased.

> "Sometimes it is said that man cannot be trusted with
> the government of himself. Can he, then be trusted with the
> government of others? Or have we found angels in the form of
> kings to govern him? Let history answer this question."
> ~ Thomas Jefferson

CHAPTER 5

PRIMARY AND SECONDARY POWER

"When the people fear their government, there is tyranny;
when the government fears the people, there is liberty."
~ Thomas Jefferson

"We hold these truths to be self-evident, that all men are created equal, that they are endowed by their Creator with certain unalienable rights, that among these are life, liberty and the pursuit of happiness."

The above sentence, found within the US Declaration of Independence, establishes one-half of the formula for how freedom works in the United States. It dethroned Kings from being the middlemen in-between God and the People. It established that all of mankind were created by and centralized under God. It acknowledged that we were endowed with talents, gifts, power and Rights from the Creator. The Declaration then continues to explain that Government was created to secure (protect) God-given Rights, so that each of us would have the freedom to fulfill our destiny. Government's inability or failure to meet its obligation of protecting our God-basket would result in personal failure.

Power

Let us explore the concept of power. Without power, we would be unable to accomplish much of nothing! Power is required to convert a mental thought into a physical action. Each us is a human-like battery. Just like batteries, we all come in different physical shapes and sizes. There are baby "watch-size" type batteries, child "AAA" batteries, teenage "AA" batteries, and various adult-size batteries. The power source for our battery comes from God. He is the true source of all power. When He endows you with power, it is yours and yours alone. You become the "primary" owner and caretaker of that power (God still remains the source).

Barring technical specifics for now, our human battery is very similar to a common battery that is used to power up various electronics. Our human battery consists of such things as cells, electrolytes, acids, etc. Throughout the day, we use energy (power) to perform various actions and tasks. The more we do, the more power we need. As our power depletes over time, we must re-energize our "battery" with food, water and ample rest. Without these essentials, our battery would drain and we would not be as productive in our daily tasks. If we deny our battery these essential things for an extended period of time, it will completely drain and eventually shutdown or die. Therefore, it is important that you nurture your battery on a daily basis. However, there comes a time when we would like to physically accomplish more tasks throughout the day than our battery would "normally" allow. Yet, we only have one battery and it has only so much energy and power. Besides, we can only be in one physical location at any given moment. Therefore, how do we accomplish more within a day that our time would allow? The answer is "Secondary" power.

Secondary power

A "secondary" power is anyone or anything that has been given both a responsibility and a portion of power from the "primary" holder. For example, whenever you delegate a responsibility or task to someone, you must give them some amount of your authority and power in order for them to complete the task. The amount of power you give them should be proportionate to the task at hand. If it is a simple task, then they should only receive a small portion of your power to complete it. If a larger task or responsibility is required, so is a larger amount of your power. (If you ever want to guarantee that someone fails at something, give him or her a task but not enough power to accomplish it). Once you have delegated a task to someone and given them the appropriate amount of your power, they become the "secondary" holder of "your" power. If at a later time you consent to them delegating a portion of that task and your power to someone else, that third person becomes a "tertiary" holder of your initial power - and so on. It is extremely important to remember that while the task or responsibility is being performed, those doing the work are holding a

44

portion of "your" original power, which you got from God. Thus, you have a moral obligation of watching over and protecting what God has given you - always protect the things in your God-basket. Now, considering those holding your power also have their "own" primary power from God, there is a great chance that they will try to retain and use your power as if it was their own, thus growing their overall power base. In other words, if not kept in check, "secondary" power will start believing that "your" power is actually "theirs" and will refuse to return it, whether the initial task was completed or not. If a portion of your power is lost to this person, your power base literally becomes weaker. Your God-basket - the one needed to fulfill your purpose - comes up a little lighter in the "power" category. Eventually, those holding your power, and most likely the power of others, become so strong in their power base that they start making demands of you! (Sounds like our current Government). Little by little, they continue to claim and drain your God-given power as their own until you and your power are snuffed out. This is why it is important to keep a watchful eye and a tight reign on those who have a portion of your power. If distributed too much in any one person or thing or distributed too thinly among many, you eventually become powerless. Fortunately, if you have lost too much of your power, there is a way to replenish it; you go back to the power source - God. God remains where He has always been.

Here are the steps for distributing and protecting your God-given power from secondary power sources:

1. delegate a task or responsibility to secondary power.

2. establish a contract (tangible or implied) establishing the rules and boundaries.

3. only distribute just enough of your power needed for them to complete the job.

4. the more power you distribute, the closer and more frequent you monitor that particular secondary power.

5. if they try to grow their power beyond the initial contract, immediately terminate the relationship and reclaim your power.

Based on the above scenario, we are all familiar with situations in which secondary power was left unchecked and got too big. The cost, as always, was at the expense of the person holding the primary power. We have seen this in situations where clients have suffered great financial losses because they delegated too much of their financial responsibilities (power) to another, only never to "check-in" for a check-up. Every time we delegate a task or responsibility to someone, they become a secondary power. This primary/secondary relationship can be as short as a few minutes or it could last for years.

Government as a secondary power

Government is a secondary power. This is supported in the Declaration of Independence:

> "That to secure these rights, governments are instituted among men, deriving their just powers from the consent of the governed."

In the above statement:

- Government (secondary power) is delegated the responsibility of protecting the Rights of the People (primary power), given to them by God (source of power).

- Government (secondary power) must have the consent of the People (primary power).

- The tangible contract written to keep the secondary power of Man's-Government in check is the US Constitution.

- One of the most important methods we use to keep Government in check is with our vote.

Based on the above statement, the Government has the responsibility of protecting our Rights and we, the People, are supposed to keep Government from going beyond that role. Considering that Government has since grown beyond that responsibility and now behaves as a surrogate parent, it is quite clear that we, the People, have failed in keeping it in check. Government, our secondary power, has assumed our power from God and now dictates to us. To reiterate the quote from above:

> *"When the people fear their government, there is tyranny;*
> *when the government fears the people, there is liberty."*
> ~ *Thomas Jefferson*

The Framers of the Constitution understood the concept of primary and secondary power and created the Constitution as a way to keep Government restrained, even if the People failed to do so. As we tear down this protective document, normally through complacency, arrogance and ignorance, we remove the layers of protection in-between Government (secondary power) and the People (primary power). This is why the US Constitution is so important and will never be obsolete. It was not written to address a specific time period. It was written to address human nature and mankind's insatiable lust and quest for power. Understanding this potential danger, the Framers used the Constitution to distribute power both horizontally and vertically across Government and the People, so that no one person would have too much of it (recall King George III). The horizontal distribution of power was across the three branches of government - the executive, legislative and judicial. The vertical distribution was between the several layers of Government (Federal, State and local) and the People. The biggest base of power was to be concentrated within the People, not at the federal level of Government. Unfortunately, we have unknowingly transferred more of our power to Government and now serve it, rather than it serving us. Most power is now concentrated and centralized at the federal level of Government and decentralized in the hands of the People. Like all secondary powers not kept in check, Government will eventually consume the People, literally taking our power and eventually our lives in the process. This is the natural progression. Governments with great amounts of centralized power have killed more of its citizens in peacetime than in all of the wars combined in history. This can only happen when the People (primary power) fail to keep Man's-government (secondary power) in check. The Constitution was written to keep handcuffs on the federal Government, not the People. It was put in place to help to preserve your Rights and power from God. To clarify, the use of secondary power is a necessity. When utilized correctly, it offers great benefits and allows each of us to get more things accomplished than otherwise. Each one of us uses and are used as forms of secondary power several times throughout the day. It allows us to delegate a task that we normally would or could do ourselves to someone else. Teachers are secondary powers that educate our children. Those on security patrol within your neighborhood are secondary power. Secondary powers are needed, just ensure that you keep them in check.

Because secondary power is derived from primary power, if the primary power goes away, so does the secondary power. This is a litmus test for determining if something or someone is a secondary power. Using the examples above, if parents withdrew their children from school, the teachers for that school would no longer have students to teach, therefore their responsibility would go away. If everyone moved out of their community, there would be nothing left to patrol. There are several forms of secondary power around you at any given time. Some examples include:

Teachers	Restaurant waiters/servers
Taxicab drivers	Police/security officers
Dry cleaner	Housekeepers
Landscapers	Home care providers
Coworker	Government

When you delegate a responsibility to someone and give him or her a portion of your power needed to accomplish the goal, then they are to serve you. You do not serve them.

Recall, the initial responsibility of Government was to protect our Rights from God. In exchange, we are willing to give a small portion of that power to do so. However, as the responsibilities of Government grow, so must its powers. If left to grow, eventually Government would have most of the responsibility and therefore most of our power. This scenario is termed the "Nanny" state. Just like a Nanny, the government becomes our provider, surrogate parent and caretaker. The irony is that the very power it is using to do so came directly from God. The People it was given to, now under Government control, became careless with it.

The Flow of Power

The flow of power operates as such:

1. God (the source) endows you with power

2. You (primary holder) loan a portion of that power to someone else (secondary power)

3. They, in turn, loan a portion of your power to another (tertiary power)

Anytime this power hierarchy becomes out of order, you will have problems. God must always remain above the primary and the primary must always remain the secondary and so on. We do not empower God - He empowers us. This is illustrated in picture #8.

Picture #8

Independence lost through power redistribution

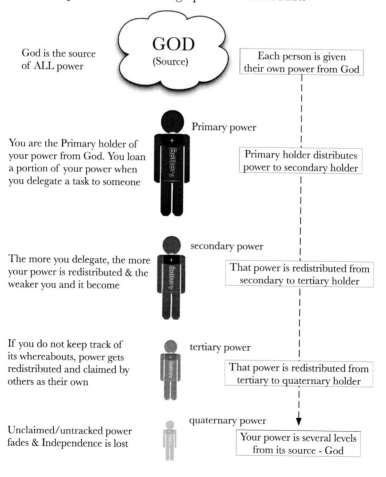

Remember, your power came from God, so it is not technically yours to permanently give away to others. It is on loan to you from God, so you can temporarily extend the loan at best. To lose your God-given power comes with great consequences. A person without power cannot obtain independence and thus cannot take risks and therefore cannot grow. Without growth, you cannot steer your ship towards your purpose or destiny. If you find yourself in any of these scenarios, you are strongly encouraged to immediately seek God. He is the source of ALL power and can replenish you with it.

It is important to allow every individual to grow his or her own God-given power. When a child becomes old enough to attempt to tie his or her shoes, they are attempting to exercise their God-given power. It is their individual power. Without cultivating this power, they will become dependent upon others. This is one example of many. We, as Christians, must not use Government to stifle the powers of others, just because we disagree on how it is used. If they are using their power in ways that interfere with our God-given Rights, then it is the legitimate responsibility of Government to step in, as stated in our Declaration of Independence. Otherwise, it is theirs, on loan from God.

Considering Government is a secondary power, implies that people with positions within the Government are supposed to serve the People. Whenever the power of Government grows larger than that of the People there will be problems. Again, this is because the hierarchy of power has been reversed. This does not mean that specific individuals within Government positions are literal servants (i.e. slaves) to its citizens. It means that their particular position represents a duty of servitude to the People. Remember, their very paychecks are paid from private-sector dollars (taxes). When you pay someone to perform a service, you are the employer, not the employee. This position must be maintained throughout the life of the job or service.

Takeaways:

- Government is a secondary power, established to protect each individual's (primary power) Rights from God (power source).

- We, the People, delegate responsibilities, give consent and a portion of our power to government, in order for it to fulfill its duties.

- Secondary power must always be kept in check. If not, it will grow and assume the role of primary power.

- Those things void of power either slow down or die.

- The further power gets away from its source (God), the more diluted and ineffective it becomes.

- To reclaim your primary power, seek the source of all power - God.

Power gets weaker as it moves away from its initial source. However, Government's power is getting stronger. This should be an indication that we are going in the wrong direction by growing Government even more. When the natural flow of power gets out of order, dysfunction sets in. In these, and other similar situations, the resolution is to reestablish the correct flow of power.

CHAPTER 6

THE BLUE & RED CONCEPT

"Men, in a word, must necessarily be controlled, either by a
power within them, or by a power without them; either by the
Word of God, or by the strong arm of man; either by the Bible,
or by the bayonet." ~ Robert Winthrop

Are you Blue or Red?

The Blue and Red concept is just a simple way of using colors to identify whether you are operating under the ways of God or under the ways of Man/Government; either under freedom or enslavement, respectively. Note - the colors are for clarity and are in no way associated with the colors of the Democrat or Republican Party.

Blue represents God's-government - the more blue you become, the more you are moving towards God and freedom.

Red represents Government and/or Man - the more red you become, the more you are moving towards Government and enslavement.

Now, you cannot simply profess that you are Blue or Red, on the side of God or Man, respectively. You identify yourself with a simple litmus test, defined by the methods of God, which include:

- morality

- virtues

- conscience

- principles

- commandments

The methods of God are "internal" to you. They operate within you, guiding your internal compass using morality, virtues, conscience, principles and commandments. If you tend to operate under the methods of Man, then you are more Red than Blue. The methods of Man include, but are not limited to:

- force

- fear

- debt

- dependency

The methods of Man are "external" to you. Rather than being guided by your "internal" compass under God, your path is "externally" forced by other people or Government.

Because the concept of Blue and Red represent freedom and force, they contradict each other and are on sliding scales. The more Blue you become, the less Red (enslaved) you are. Recall that God is the source of love, freedom and all things that are good. Therefore, when you operate under His methods of "internal" government, you become "Blue" and move towards freedom. Now, because no two people are alike, each of us will be made up of different parts of Blue and Red. Because we are imperfect, no human being can become completely Blue. That designation is reserved for Angels. Using the above litmus test, we know Man's-government falls under the category of Red, because Government operates by force. Not only that, but Government also creates fear, debt and dependency, so when you increase grow Government, you get more of these things.

Note - although Government, as an institution, operates in the Red, it does not mean that those within government positions are automatically considered "Red" people by simply working for the Government. As a matter of fact, the more "Blue" people we have within Government, the more accountable Government becomes.

So, why is the concept of Blue and Red so important? It is important because those people who operate in the Blue are able to govern themselves accordingly. It is best to surround yourself with "Blue" people. Their morals, virtues and principles will rub off on you and positively influence you in those times when you are going into the Red. Conversely, "red" people drag you down, because they bring fear, force, dependency and other vices into your circle. Since Government is a huge Red, it will drag you down faster than anything. If at all possible, place boundaries on your relationships with Government and Red people and you will see your life naturally move back into the Blue. Blue begets Blue and Red begets Red. Picture #9 represents someone who is living under the methods of God. It means that they are living under God's morality, virtues, principles and commandments. They have a very high conscience and accountability to God. They are very "blue," with very little red in their lives.

Picture #9

Someone living under a large amount of God's-government

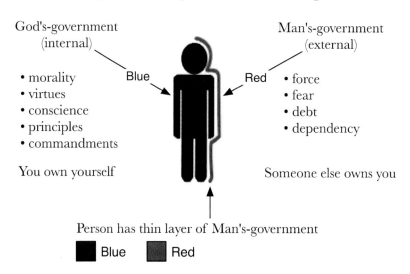

God's-government (internal)		Man's-government (external)
• morality	Blue Red	• force
• virtues		• fear
• conscience		• debt
• principles		• dependency
• commandments		
You own yourself		Someone else owns you

Person has thin layer of Man's-government

■ Blue   ▨ Red

God wants each of us to operate in the "blue," under His morality, virtues, principles and commandments. When we do, things such as fear, debt, force and dependency keep their distance, as they cannot operate within the very same space and time as those things that are of God. For example, you cannot be both fearful and have true faith in God's protection at the same time. The moment you find yourself getting away from the Blue methods of God, those Red traits start easing their way into your life. The more our Government legislates the presence of God out of society, the more it shifts from Blue to Red - from freedom to enslavement. Picture #10 represents someone who is under the enslavement of such things as force, fear, vices, debt, dependency, addiction, etc.

Picture #10

Someone living under a large amount of Man's-government

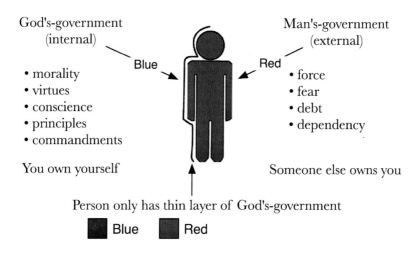

God's-government (internal)

Blue

Man's-government (external)

Red

- morality
- virtues
- conscience
- principles
- commandments

- force
- fear
- debt
- dependency

You own yourself

Someone else owns you

Person only has thin layer of God's-government

Blue   Red

"Religion and virtue are the only foundations, not only of all free government, but of social felicity under all governments and in all the combinations of human society."
~ John Adams

Each time someone Red enters into your life, not only do they bring in their own enslavement, they add to whatever enslavement you may already be dealing with. Picture #11 represents someone who has added other "Red" people to their life.

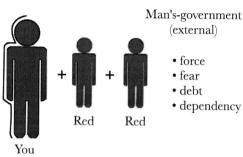

Picture #11

Adding more red people to your life

Man's-government (external)

• force
• fear
• debt
• dependency

Red   Red

You

The more red people you add to your life, the more Man's-government they bring with them

The more Red people you have in-between you and God, the harder it becomes to be independent and free. This is because their Redness literally "blocks" your path to God. Therefore, identify those Red people around you and keep them at a distance, if at all possible. Afterwards, work on removing the Redness out of your life in order to get yourself back into the Blue. This will allow you to better assist other Red people. The goal is to get as many people in society to Blue, but this must be accomplished in the ways of God, not Man. The good thing is that since Blue people represent the methods of God, they are capable of positively influencing Red people, although the process may take some time.

How does the Blue/Red concept relate to the Christian? - When we vote to grow the authority of Government, we are effectively voting more "Red" into society, which is closely followed by debt, fear, force and dependency. These types of vices enslave society. As Christians, we should be actively pointing people towards God and His morality, independence, virtues and principles.

Now, using the Blue/Red concept, let us review and translate the quote at the beginning of this chapter:

> *"Men, in a word, must necessarily be controlled, either by a power within them, or by a power without them; either by the Word of God, or by the strong arm of man; either by the Bible, or by the bayonet." ~ Robert Winthrop*

Translation:

> Because we are imperfect, each one of us must absolutely be governed over; however, we can either choose to "internally" govern ourselves under the ways of God (i.e. commandments, virtues, morality and principles) or can expect to be "externally" governed via the force of Man; we have a choice to either govern ourselves by the Bible (God) or be governed by guns (Man).

Takeaways:

- Strive to be as Blue as you can be - it removes the Red.

- As you strive to become Blue, do not cast others into the Red of Government by voting more of it into society.

Keep in mind that one of the objectives of this book is to expose the hidden battle between God's-government and Man's-government. That is to say that the more we move towards God's way of doing things, the more independent and prosperous we become as a society. On the surface, that might seem a bit obvious to most, but the battle that is raging is not being fought above-ground and out in the open. It cannot be seen with the naked eye. It is based on fundamental principles. This is the very reason Man's-government is gaining ground. The Blue/Red concept offers a way to visually identify those Blue/Red people around you and show how Government operates in the Red.

CHAPTER 7

THE PATH TO FREEDOM

"Freedom is not a gift bestowed upon us by other men, but a right that belongs to us by the laws of God and nature."
~ Benjamin Franklin

The concept of freedom is pretty straightforward. Freedom comes when you are no longer under the forced control or enslavement of others or yourself. The concept is that simple. The hard part, however, is recognizing if and when you are enslaved:

"I freed a thousand slaves. I could have freed a thousand more if only they knew they were slaves."
~ Harriet Tubman

Chattel and Indentured slavery

There are basically two forms of slavery - enslavement of the physical body (chattel slavery) and enslavement of the mind (indentured slavery). When we think of slavery, we most often think of chattel slavery. We have visions of someone being physically bound by chains or shackles. This is the easiest type of slavery to recognize, because it involves some level of physical force that you can easily visualize. Indentured slavery, on the other hand, is the hardest to recognize and escape from, because there are no outright visual signs of force. The enslavement operates "internally" - it is enslavement of the mind. It often comes in the form of verbal threats or enticements. Man's-government utilizes both chattel and indentured slavery as methods to control its citizens.

The previous Harriet Tubman quote deals with indentured slavery of the mind. In other words, if someone does not believe they are enslaved, then it is very difficult to convince them that they need to be freed of something. This is the current state of society. Because people are not physically bound, most believe they are free. However, freedom, in terms of mobility, and freedom, in terms of dependency are hardly the same. It is easier to entice someone than it is to force them. This is why Christians can't be Democrats. The Democrat-advocated entitlement programs are the worse forms of indentured slavery. They create a dependency that is much more difficult to escape than chattel forms. With the implementation of certain Government entitlements, traditional chattel slavery has been resurrected as current-day indentured slavery:

Traditional "chattel" slavery (utilized force and fear to control).

The masters gave slaves:

- Housing

- Food

- Healthcare

Current "indentured" slavery (utilizes enticements to control).

Our Government "masters" give us:

- Housing

- Food

- Healthcare

The current-day indentured model has created more indentured slaves than the traditional model ever could have imagined! Because Government only operates out of force, each time it enters into a particular situation, it brings enslavement with it. That enslavement may be chattel or indentured. Chattel slavery would be any law that demands some type of action of you, followed by physical force if you do not comply. Indentured slavery would be any law that entices citizens to come under the authority or dependency of Government. Because most people do not openly see indentured slavery within Government programs and/or laws, they are more easily duped into being supportive of such. As Christians, we should not be advocating such dependencies. There is no such thing as free-enslavement or enslaved-freedom.

Your path to freedom

The only thing that can truly enslave and force you against your will is other people. Think about it - if you were the last person on the planet, whom would you be enslaved to, other than potentially yourself? If you wanted to do something, who would be there to stop or restrict you? No one! This is the simple premise of freedom. "Freedom" is freeing yourself from the force of Man. You accomplish freedom by dislodging any person(s) that has lodged themselves in-between you and the source of freedom - God. However, we often get in our own way, enslaving ourselves in the process. Therefore, the next time you claim that others are enslaving you, first ensure that "they" are not "you." If you are enslaved, however, then tackle those enslavements (i.e. fear, debt, dependency, hate, addiction) by operating out of God's principles and virtues. The aim is to get closer to God by removing the proverbial internal and external chains that bind you. God has given us several methods to accomplish such feats. Unfortunately, we continue to reject them out of arrogance, replacing them with "Man-solutions," which have proven to fail.

Recall, God is the source of love and therefore He is the source of freedom. This is because freedom is one of the characteristics of love. God encourages us to become free and has given us the power of love to do so; that is love for others and love for thyself. To acquire this given blessing, you must seek God, for He is the source of both. There is no human being or thing that can offer you the freedom that God can. Therefore, when you place or allow things to come in-between you and God, you are creating a blockade to the very blessings God has in store for you.

It is very essential that you establish a clear, unobstructed path to God. The clearer your path to the Source, the better off your life will be in general. To reiterate, an enslaved person cannot take risks and without risks you cannot grow and without growth, you cannot obtain independence. Thus, identify those individuals who bring force and vices into your life and keep them at a safe distance. This does not mean that you cannot help them, if they choose to be helped. Just do not let them come in-between you and God during the process. Since Government operates out of force, it fails to qualify as Godly and must be kept at a distance too - never embraced. Be careful not to invite Man's-Government back into your life, under the premise that it will do Christ-like things. Remember, you cannot move closer to God with Government or Man-force in the way of your path (picture #12).

Picture #12

Path to Freedom

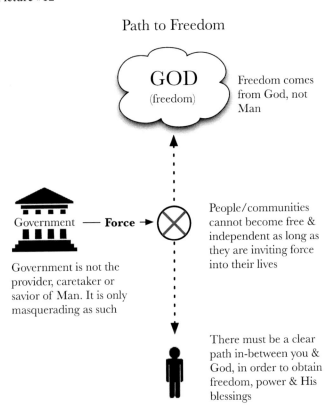

GOD (freedom)

Freedom comes from God, not Man

Government — **Force** ⊗

Government is not the provider, caretaker or savior of Man. It is only masquerading as such

People/communities cannot become free & independent as long as they are inviting force into their lives

There must be a clear path in-between you & God, in order to obtain freedom, power & His blessings

Government's "force" field

Because freedom (God) and force (Man's-government) cannot occupy the very same space at the very same time, the more we increase Man's-government, the more immoral and destructive society will become. This is because the force that Government brings with it acts as a "force" field, shielding out

God and His goodness (i.e. morality, abundance, independence and love). Have you noticed that ever since Governments across the world have united as a way to propose solutions, the worse off we have become? Worldwide Government summits may be held with good intentions, but the end result is that more of Man's-government and its force is introduced into the world. This increased force acts like a force field, literally blocking the earth, and all things within it, from receiving God's blessings. This is diagramed in picture #13.

Picture #13

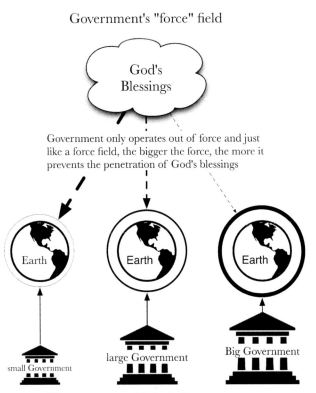

Government's "force" field

God's Blessings

Government only operates out of force and just like a force field, the bigger the force, the more it prevents the penetration of God's blessings

Earth

Earth

Earth

small Government

large Government

Big Government

The more we seek Man's-Government,
the less God can work in the situation

Takeaways:

- God represents the ultimate love, thus the ultimate freedom.

- God is the source of love, independence, abundance, freedom and power.

- Man's-government does not offer freedom; it enslaves you.

- To become free, dislodge all forms of force from in-between you and God.

- The force of Government acts as a force field, literally shielding out God's blessings.

Freedom does not come from Man - it comes from God. When we increase the power of Government, regardless of its good intentions, a layer of force is added in-between society and God. Government's role is to protect freedom, not try to provide it. Love is the path to freedom. It is by no coincidence that those who have used love throughout history to combat the evils of mankind were successful. This is because God is love and He is the Master. This is also why evil can only prevail for so long. Love is one of several tools that we have been given to address our challenges. This is the "method" of Christ and as Christians (Christ-like), we should always look to exercise love in lieu of force.

CHAPTER 8

THE TRANSITIVE EQUALITY OF CHRIST

*"How many observe Christ's birthday! How few his precepts! O!
'tis easier to keep holidays than commandments."*
~ Benjamin Franklin

Do you recall the following formula?

If A = B and B = C, then A = C

Is it called the "Transitive Property of Equality." It states that if we know for a fact that "A equals B and B equals C, then A must equal C." It is based on the premise of equality. If we apply this same formula for what we know about Christ, it would read as follows:

Christ = Love and Love = Freedom, then Christ = Freedom

If most of us had to sum up all of the qualities of Christ in one word, that word would most likely be love. Christ is "love." Like Christ, when you love someone, you exhibit such things as forgiveness, understanding, support, care, patience, consideration and encouragement. These are some of the many characteristics of love. They tag along with love, regardless of where it may go. However, these characteristics alone are not enough to define love. True love is established when it is accompanied with freedom. Because God truly loves us, He gives us freedom. In other words, love cannot exist without freedom. This is one of the key reasons why Christians can't be Democrats. It is not because the Democrats are incapable of love - sure they are. The reason why Christians can't be Democrats is because many Christians support the Democrat Party because of its "public relations" stance of wanting to help those in need, especially the poor. This gives the Democrat Party the "appearance" of being Christ-like in its efforts. This is the "bait" the Party uses to hook so many people and Christians. However, this is far from the truth! Government operates out of force, which is not a characteristic of love, therefore, not a representation of Christ.

To better show this, let's apply the transitive formula of equality (If A = B and B = C, then A = C) to both Government and Christ:

Government = Force and Force = Enslavement, thus Government = Enslavement

Now, compare this again with the transitive equalities of Christ:

Christ = Love and Love = Freedom, thus Christ = Freedom

Clearly the transitive properties of Government and Christ are not one in the same. They are opposites. Therefore, to use Man's-government as a means to fulfill the love and compassionate nature of Christ is actually a gross misrepresentation of Him. If we aspire to be "Christ-like," then not only should we exhibit love, we should promote its greatest characteristic - freedom. We must allow people to be free in their decisions, as long as those decisions do not interfere with the Rights of others. We must stop using Government as a means to enforce God's morality upon others. Besides, who are we to force others when we, ourselves, are not forced by God? Hypothetically, if God were to force morality upon mankind, then we would all go to Heaven for sure! Can you guarantee that your use of Government force would accomplish the same results?

> "The people never give up their liberties but
> under some delusion." ~ Edmund Burke

> "The true danger is when liberty is nibbled away,
> for expedience, and by parts." ~ Edmund Burke

The Patriot, the Dictator and the Hypocrite

In regards to Freedom, there are basically three types of people:

- those who believe in freedom for all - the **patriot**

- those who believe in freedom for none - the **dictator**

- those who believe in freedom for some - the **hypocrite**

Based on the three, it is quite apparent that Christ was not a dictator nor hypocrite. Therefore, being "Christ-like," neither should we. It is guaranteed that some people will choose to engage in behaviors that you may personally disagree with or exercise their God-given Rights in a manner not consistent with being "Christ-like." One of the hardest things the Christian patriot must learn to accept and respect is that such behaviors are a consequence of freedom. I'm not suggesting that you advocate or condone such behavior, but only to accept it as their individual choice. If, however, you want to ensure that no one engages in "ungodly" ways, then you must certainly enslave everyone. Yet, who are you to do so? Such a righteous position puts you in the category of the hypocrite, only allowing freedom for those whose actions and/or beliefs you approve of. That is not freedom - that is force! We must resist the temptation to enslave others under the long arm of Government simply because we disagree on how they are living their personal lives. If you claim to be a Christian, then act like a patriot and advocate and promote freedom under God, rather than enslavement under Man's-government. As Christians, our greatest enemy is not necessarily the atheist. It is the dictator and the hypocrite. Of the patriot, the dictator or the hypocrite - which are you?

WWJND? (What Would Jesus NOT Do?)

"What Would Jesus Do (WWJD)?" is one of the most misguided rhetorical questions you could ask someone when it comes to political policy. It implies that the Government is somehow justified in its actions, based on what Jesus would do if presented with the same scenario. For example:

- Jesus would help the poor; therefore, Government should help the poor.

- Jesus would not condone greed; therefore, Government should not condone greed.

- Jesus would heal the sick; therefore, Government should get involved with healthcare.

- Jesus would share his blessings; therefore, Government should share its blessings (recall, it has none).

- Jesus would "fill in the blank"; therefore, Government should "fill in the blank."

Recall, a thought and its associated action is a two-part process. Performing one without the other would represent an incomplete process. We have all been guilty of acting on something without thinking or thinking without acting upon it. This is what we need to remember when trying to place Christ within a political party or ideology. To say, "this is how Jesus would have thought" without also reflecting upon the methods He would have used to "act" upon that thought, would represent one-half of the equation. Doing so would be a misrepresentation of Jesus. We already know that Government is force and that Jesus is *not* force. This means that Government and Jesus contradict each other. Therefore, "what would Jesus do?" is an invalid argument for dictating political policy, because we know He would not use force to act out His thoughts. A better question would be "what would Jesus NOT do (WWJND)?" Again, we know that He would not use force. This is because one of the end-results of force is that it pushes people away. Surely, this was not what Jesus represented. Conversely, if you want to attract people, you use love. Our attraction to Jesus is out of mutual love. Therefore, we should never delegate our Christian duties to Government out of convenience. The methods of Christ belong in the hands of the individual Christian. The duty is ours. It does not matter how many Christian voters give their consent to pass on their responsibilities to Government - it still remains an individual, Christian effort.

"The doctrines of Jesus are simple, and tend all
to the happiness of man." ~ Thomas Jefferson

Takeaways:

- Christ = Love and Love = Freedom, thus Christ = Freedom.

- Government (force) is the opposite of Christ (freedom).

- God does not force you, so who are you to force others in the name of God?

- We don't know exactly what Jesus would do, but we do know what He would not do - He would not use force.

- Being "Christ-like" is *your* duty, not Government's.

- Love attracts (pulls); Force pushes.

It is important that we do not use the concept of "what would Jesus do" as justification to vote in a Government Theocracy (officials governing by divine guidance). Such a theocracy would force Christian beliefs upon others. It is a very dangerous stance to take. It could encourage other religious groups to do the same. If we expect society to get better, we must educate others of the ways of God and methods of Christ - not force it upon them. Force will only brings resistance.

If the word of God has given you the conviction and inspiration to use the force of Man to accomplish His will, then you have already contradicted what it means to be "Christ-like." Government is not the path to righteousness. As Christians, we should never look towards Government to do the will of God. Problems are not solved with force - they are solved with love. Neither God nor Christ needs a Government sidekick.

CHAPTER 9

CHRIST, THE ANARCHIST

*"Resistance to tyranny becomes the Christian and social duty of
each individual ... Continue steadfast and, with a proper sense
of your dependence on God, nobly defend those rights which
heaven gave, and no man ought to take from us."*
~ John Hancock

*"What is government itself but the greatest of all reflections on
human nature? If men were angels, no government would be
necessary. If angels were to govern men, neither external nor
internal controls on government would be necessary."*
~ James Madison

Christ, if gauged on the political left-right spectrum, would be aligned to
the extreme political right - not the political left, as many people argue. This
is easily determined by what we already know about God, Christ and Angels -
that they all operate completely "opposite" of Man's-government. We also know
that as political parties move from left to right on the spectrum, they move
from an extreme amount of Man's-government (totalitarianism) to a complete
absence of Man's-government (anarchy). For this reason alone, Christ could
not be politically left. He could not possibly be aligned with totalitarianism
or those political parties whose policies require more influence of Man's-government in our lives than God's-government (His Father's way). Christ, would
align with the political concept of anarchy (absence of Man's-government/au-
thority). This is shown in picture #14.

Picture #14

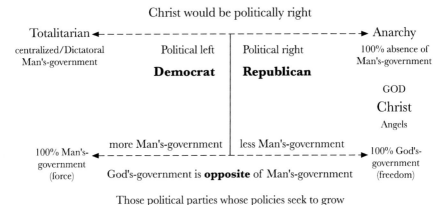

Those political parties whose policies seek to grow
Man's-government are moving opposite of Christ

Based on the diagram of the political spectrum, as political parties move right-to-left on the political spectrum, they move "away" from God, Christ and Angels (God-government). As you can see, the methods of Christ and those political parties on the left are opposite of each other. Many Christians get sucked into the Democrat Party's message of "what" Christ would do, while completely ignoring the amounts of Man's-government required to accomplish it. However, if you were to ask them if Christ would condone using force, fear, stealing from others or removing God-given Rights to accomplish God's will, they would answer "no." However, this is exactly what the Democrat Party is doing. As a matter of fact, all political parties utilize some level of Man's-government (recall, that is Government's purpose), but Christians should not be supporting parties whose polices actively grow Man's-government. Those political parties that fall under the political-left are the Fascist, Communist, Socialist, Green, Liberal and Democrat parties.

This is why Christians can't be Democrats. On the political spectrum, the Democrat Party is to the "left" of the Republican Party. Not only that, the Democrat party seeks to be a secondary "Source" to God (the "true" Source). It attempts to be the provider to God's people. However, we do not need a secondary source. This only creates competition. God does fine on His own. Instead of trying to become a secondary source, Man's-government should stick to being the "force" that protects the Source (God), as its stated role in our Declaration of Independence. If we would only protect the Source to begin with, then a secondary Man-based source would not be necessary. Again, the Democrat's overall motivation is to do good for mankind by using the force of Man's-government to accomplish it. However, if they would only channel that same motivation through God's-government instead, most of this book would be a moot point.

Also, we do not need to spend a lot of time debating where Christ would stand politically on controversial issues, such as abortion, homosexuality, war, helping the poor, healthcare, capital punishment, etc. Tens of thousands of life-hours and extreme amounts of money have gone into researching such criteria, only to have "experts" disagree over the findings, wasting our time in the process. These topics are too subjective, superficial and will always remain argumentative. Such subjective and superficial discussions continue to divide Christians politically. We use them to debate where Christ would fall on the political spectrum based on social conscience (a sense of responsibility or concern for the problems and injustices of society) as the focal point. Yet, our individual beliefs on social conscience issues are subjective too. They are heavily influenced by our personal past, beliefs and emotional ties to the topic at hand. Therefore, we must go deeper than surface level conversations to become politically yoked. That underlying conversation should be between God's-government and Man's-government (freedom and force, respectively). Very few Christians can argue on where Christ would operate if given a choice between God's-government and Man's-government. This is why this particular criteria is the strongest of them all.

Regardless of where someone thinks Christ would be aligned politically, no political party can monopolize its claim on Christ. As a matter of speaking, there is very little chance that He would be affiliated with any political party at all. This is because every political party uses some level of force to accomplish its goals and Christ would not condone using any amount of force to govern over Man. However, this does not mean that we cannot get "politically "closer to Christ via our party affiliation. Although we cannot operate under 100% of God's-government, Christians should strive to move towards the political right, closer to where God, Christ and Angels reside. We can never get perfectly aligned with Christ politically, because some form of Government is needed in society.

Takeaways:

- Anarchy (absence of Man's-government) is to the extreme political right. This is where Christ can be found, because He is opposite of Man's-government.

- Political parties should be measured by the amount of force they want to use on society, not by their subjective thoughts on social issues.

- The more we move politically-left towards Man's-government, the more we move away from God's-government.

- You cannot get to God through Man. Likewise, you cannot get to God's-government byway of Man's-government.

Considering that we win each time we utilize God's-government, we are doing God a disservice when we vote for those political parties that seek more of Man's-government. The Founders understood that only God can deliver the things that we need and that Man's-government, at best, could only use its force to protect the "distribution channels" of His blessings. In other words, if God is delivering financial blessings, then Man's-government should be the armored truck. God is the provider - Government is the protector of His provisions. Man's-government was never intended to be the source of provisions. Both God and Government cannot be the source of your provisions. Who is currently playing "God" in your life?

Love is the answer to all of our problems. Because God is the source of love, whenever we utilize love in any situation, He automatically comes with it and is present in the act of loving. Because we already know that Man is no match for God, whenever we operate out of love and God's-government, we prevail each time. This is what He promised us. Conversely, Man's-government is force. Thus, it can never create laws that embodies love. New laws that attempt to promote love can be passed each year, but it would still be out of reach. In other words, the moment you seek Man's-government to enact laws of love, abundance, equality, fairness or any other moral deed, is the very moment you looked in the wrong direction. If you do not agree, take a quick look at your bookmark/list - these things come from God.

CHAPTER 10

WHY CHRISTIANS CAN'T
BE DEMOCRATS

*"My reading of history convinces me that most bad
government results from too much government."*
~ *Thomas Jefferson*

"Christian" - pertaining to, or derived from Jesus Christ or His teachings; a Christian faith.

A Christian should strive to be "Christ-like." The concept of why Christians can't be Democrats is a philosophical exploration, based on the universal principle of "Freedom vs. Force." Freedom being defined as "freedom from Man" and Force being defined as "forced against your will."

So, why can't Christians be Democrats? One of the main reasons is because the Democrat Party advocates utilizing Man's-government as a means to help provide for those citizens who are in need (this is probably the huge draw many Christians have to the Democrat Party). As strange as it may sound, the reason why Christians can't be Democrats has little to do about helping people, but more about where the help is coming from. Before going forward, let me be very clear - Yes, helping people is absolutely what God would want us to do, but He never intended for us to accomplish this through force. How do we know this? Well, we know this because God, Himself, is not force. On the contrary, Man's-government operates out of force and therefore is opposite of God. This being the case, it should not be actively viewed nor promoted by Christians as an institution to do God's will. An increase in Man's-government should be a sad occasion for Christians, not a joyous one. This is because an increase in Man's-government effectively increases its power and force. It uses that newfound power, that initially came from God, to bring more force upon its citizens via new laws, regulations and mandates. However, God gave us, the People, that same power so that "we" could do His will. He did not intend for us transfer it to Government for it to fulfill his commandments. When you add force to a command, it becomes a demand (this concept is covered in Chapter 13). Recall, Man's-government is what we get when God's-government fails. However, Man's-government should always be a reactionary and temporary response to God's-government, never a proactive and permanent alternative. This is why entitlement programs are noble, but very bad ideas. Because they increase dependency, they become proactive and perpetual programs that may never go away. Entitlement programs were not initially part of our Government because they infringed upon the Rights of others. The Founders believed in a reliance upon Divine Providence (the care and superintendence which God exercises over his creatures). However, this no longer seems to be the case. Divine Providence is not Divine Government. The more we fail to do God's will as individuals, the larger Man's-government must become to compensate for that failure. When this happens, all of society suffers in the end, because the increased force that comes along with Government pushes out our freedoms and the things of God. This is scientific. As Christians, we must stop transferring our duties to Government, regardless of our good intentions to do so.

A more philosophical answer can be found within the following four things we already know to be true:

1. God

2. Man's-government

3. Principles found within God's nature

4. Political policy

1. God is the source of all things good. He is the ultimate love and therefore is the ultimate freedom (which is a characteristic of love).

2. Man's-government only operates out of force. It creates various laws, regulations and mandates and utilizes force as a way to keep everyone in compliance.

3. Nowhere on God's earth can freedom and force occupy the very same space at the very same time. Therefore, freedom and force are opposites of each other. So, when we increase Man's-government (which is force) in society, God (who is freedom) and the things of God are forcefully pushed out. Because of His ultimate love for us, God allows us the free will to push Him aside.

4. The Democrat Party, more than the Republicans, openly pushes for legislation that would increase the reach, authority and force of Man's-Government. (The biggest of these are entitlement and equality programs). Although the intentions are noble and good, God is ultimately pushed out as a result of the increased force.

For example, imagine a room that is completely full of 100% of freedom. Now, imagine that you introduce a certain amount force into that room. When you do, an equal amount of freedom must leave the room. This is because freedom and force cannot occupy the exact same space at the exact same time. Therefore, the more force you add to the room, an equal amount of freedom leaves. The concept of what happens to freedom when force enters into the room is the same thing that happens when we increase Man's-government into society. Each time more Government (force) enters society, an equal part of God's presence (freedom) and the things of God, such as love, independence, abundance and other virtues, are pushed out. Make no doubt about it; God is always in our presence. "He" never leaves or forsakes us - "We" push Him away! For example, when you are dealing with a particular challenging situation, you can either choose to address it by utilizing God's ways choose to use your own. When you choose to use your own methods, what you are essentially doing is "pushing" God's way aside for the moment. This is what we are doing when we choose to use Man's-government to deal with things rather than dealing with them using God's way. As a Christian who believes in God, you cannot move towards the ways of God while at the same time voting for a political party whose policies cause an indirect move away from Him. This is a direct contradiction.

The Founders understood the dangers that came with Government trying to help its citizens, rather than the citizens having a reliance upon God:

> *"The policy of the American government is to leave their*
> *citizens free, neither restraining nor aiding them in*
> *their pursuits." ~ Thomas Jefferson*

This is to say, Government aid to some citizens requires confiscating the Rights of others. After awhile, dependency upon Government aid becomes so great that politicians effectively end up controlling all "dependent" citizens by their "yay" or "nay" vote in Congress. Does this sound familiar?

To reiterate, Man's-government is necessary and plays an important role in our society. It is a man-made institution that uses it authority and force to deal with the imperfections of the human conscience mind. However, its role in our daily lives should remain limited, be kept on a short leash and caged up whenever possible. The global population is increasing and people are living longer. It is impossible to sustain Government aid programs much longer. Any country offering such programs will eventually collapse. It goes against the laws of God's nature. Besides, why would you want something that is opposite of God to be the provider of your needs? It is our duty as citizens, and especially Christians, to help others, not the job of Government.

The Freedom Formula

The concept of removing Government is better represented in the "Freedom Formula." The Freedom Formula is a mathematical expression stated as:

G-g=F (God - government = freedom)

Later on you will find that the expression can also be stated as:

G-f=F (God - force = Freedom)

Or, it can be written as:

G-m=F (God - man = freedom)

The Freedom formula states that in order to obtain the freedom that comes from God, you must ensure that neither the force of Government nor the force of Man (including yourself) lodges themselves in-between you and God. This concept is illustrated in picture #15 and based on the following:

Picture #15

The Freedom Formula

G-g=F (God - government = Freedom)

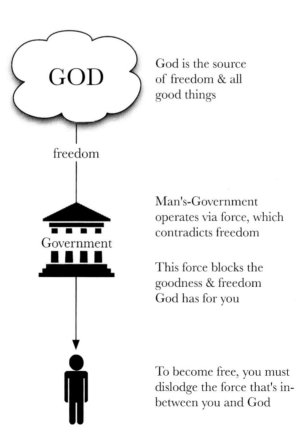

GOD — God is the source of freedom & all good things

freedom

Government — Man's-Government operates via force, which contradicts freedom

This force blocks the goodness & freedom God has for you

To become free, you must dislodge the force that's in-between you and God

God is the source of freedom

God is the source of all things that are good. He is your destination for the good things in your life. To receive His blessing at their full capacity, you must ensure that the path in-between you and God is clear and unobstructed. Anything or anyone blocking this path will cut off part or all of your blessings. Just like driving a car down a particular road, if the road becomes blocked, you cannot arrive at your destination in a timely manner. You must find an alternative route, which will cost you not only more money, but it will cost you something that you cannot get back - time. When you purposely allow Government and others to block the path in-between you and God, it robs you of your blessing and invaluable life-hours. Because of its authority, Man's-government has a natural inclination to rise above the People and lodge itself in-between the People and God, eventually intercepting and consuming the People's power and blessings from God. Literally, Government forcibly takes your finances and your power to make decisions. At this point, society falls under the rule of Man. This, my fellow Christians, is the path we are currently on. One of the biggest challenges is that it is the nature of mankind to seek out masters to place their burdens upon. Masters offer a sense of relief. There is great comfort in someone else absorbing our personal responsibilities, when we chose not to do so ourselves. Government surely knows better than us, right?

The "Independent" Christian Voter

The politically "independent" Christian voter is a misnomer. The stance of the "independent" voter is that they do not claim to be a staunch member of any particular political party and they vote for the individual politician instead of a political party as a whole. However, considering that every political party is made of different parts of God's-government and Man's-government, it would only make sense that Christians vote for the party that has the highest make-up of God's-government. In other words, why would a Christian vote for a party that represents more Man's-government than God's-government? As a Christian, you can either choose to cast your vote for one or the other, but not both. Casting your vote across party lines only cancels out your vote in the end. This is because the ideologies of the Republican and Democrat parties reflect polar opposites. One party wants to increase Government in our lives and the other wants to decrease it. It is not expected that you will agree 100% of the policies of either party, however, it is your Christian duty to vote for the party whose "methods," not necessarily beliefs, lean more towards the "methods" of Christ. Christians should be in the business of promoting freedom and not in the business of growing Man's-Government. The "independent" Christian should vote on the known principles within God's nature and universe, not on the rhetoric from the politician's tongue.

Takeaways:

- G-g=F (God minus government equals Freedom).

- Force is the enemy of freedom.

- A politically "Independent" Christian voter is an oxymoron; the vote cancels itself out.

Whenever we seek the "solutions" of Man's-government, we are effectively rejecting and pushing the solutions of God away. Again, God has already given us the solutions to the problems in the world. When we use His methods, we are better able to deal with our current circumstances. However, it is our arrogance that makes us continue to seek solutions through Man's-government, our secondary power, rather than solutions through God, our source of power. It is God's universal principle of freedom and force that states why Christians can't be Democrats. If we want to reverse the current downward spiral of society, then we must start reducing the responsibilities, authority and thus the force of Man's-government. When we do, the things of God will return. Again, this is not speculation. This is what He promised. It is the principle that holds true throughout God's universe.

THE FORCE SEPARATES
FROM THE SOURCE

CHAPTER 11

"SEPARATION OF CHURCH AND STATE"

"I have lived, Sir, a long time, and the longer I live, the more convincing proofs I see of this truth--that God Governs the affairs of men. And if a sparrow cannot fall to the ground without His notice, is it probable that an empire can rise without His aid?" ~ Benjamin Franklin

"Our constitution was made only for a moral and religious people. It is wholly inadequate to the government of any other." ~ John Adams

The phrase, "Separation of church and state" has been one of the most, if not the most, damaging phrases to our Constitutional Republic. Most everyone has heard of the phrase, yet ask someone in which of our Founding documents is the phrase located and they will most likely say the Constitution. Ask them to locate the phrase within the Constitution and they will be surprised that they cannot find it. That is because the phrase is not there, nor within any of our Founding documents. As a matter of fact, neither the words "separation" nor "church" appear anywhere within the Constitution. However, because "separation of church and state" has become part of our everyday lexicon, we have "mentally" written it into our Constitution. Anytime "separation of church and state" is uttered, people are actually mistakenly referring to the 1st Amendment of the US Constitution. Unfortunately, "separation of church and state" and the 1st Amendment have become synonymous terms, yet they are hardly the same. The 1st Amendment prevents Congress from writing laws that would establish a national religion or church, while "separation of church and state" implies that the "affairs" of churches/religion/God and Government shall not mix.

WHY CHRISTIANS CAN'T BE DEMOCRATS

The 1st Amendment

The 1st Amendment partially reads:

> "Congress shall make no law respecting an establishment of religion, or prohibiting the free exercise thereof;"

This states that Congress, at the federal level of Government, cannot create any laws that establishes a religion or any laws that would prevent anyone from exercising their particular religious beliefs or lack thereof.[1] The Framers of the Constitution wanted to ensure that the federal level of government did not create any laws that would establish an "official" religion or church, like Great Britain had in the Church of England during their time period. Without the protection of the 1st Amendment, the federal government could potentially establish an "official" national religion that would operate "top-down" and supersede and blanket the various religions throughout the nation. If such laws were created, new policies to support the religion could potentially be enforced with guns.

"Separation of church and state"

"Separation of church and state" implies that the affairs of church and government should not mix. In its current misunderstanding, "separation of church and state" eradicates God and religion out of the Government sector, which eventually enslaves each and every one of us under the rule of Man. This is because it effectively erects a proverbial wall in-between force (Government) and freedom (God). As God gets separated off, we are left to the vices and force of Men (Government). This is to our detriment and purposely sought out by those who seek God's throne. In other words, if someone aspires to become the "ruler of Men," they must first attempt to eradicate the competition - God. They must first separate society, in general, from the allegiance of their current "Master." Man's-government cannot rule over Man while being in competition with God at the same time. Recall, you cannot serve two Masters. Therefore, "separation of church and state" is Man's-government's greatest weapon, as it

---

1. What defines a particular religion can be subjective. However, recall that the role of Man's-government is to protect our Rights. Thus, if a particular religious practice conflicts with someone's Rights, Government must intervene. For example, a religious practice that calls for sacrificing someone's life would conflict with the "right to life."

can justify using laws to remove the presence of God/Christ (the competition) out of society, in general. Although we can maintain a personal belief in God, Government can now rule without any accountability to God.

Origin of the phrase

As previously mentioned, neither the word "church" nor "separation" can be found anywhere within our Constitution. So, how did the phrase come into existence? It was lifted from a reply letter that Thomas Jefferson wrote to the Danbury Baptist church, to address their concerns with Government's possible interference with religion. Here is part of that letter:

"Believing with you that religion is a matter which lies solely between Man & his God, that he owes account to none other for his faith or his worship, that the legitimate powers of government reach actions only, & not opinions, I contemplate with sovereign reverence that act of the whole American people which declared that their legislature should "make no law respecting an establishment of religion, or prohibiting the free exercise thereof," thus building a wall of separation between Church & State."

The US Supreme Court used the words "wall of separation between church and state" from Thomas Jefferson's letter to interpret the 1st Amendment to mean that the Government and churches should be separate. Never mind that Jefferson was never present during the Constitutional convention.

Using God's power to separate from Him

The concept of "separation of church and state" is a misrepresentation of what the Framers intended when drafting the 1st Amendment. The role of Government is to protect what God has given, not detach itself from God. This is stated in our Declaration of Independence:

"We hold these truths to be self-evident, that all men are created equal, that they are endowed by their Creator with certain unalienable rights, that among these are life, liberty and the pursuit of happiness. That to secure these rights, governments are instituted among men, deriving their just powers from the consent of the governed."

87

These two lines clearly establish the belief that God created mankind and endowed each of us with Rights and it is the role of government to secure (protect) those Rights from God. Now, how can Government effectively protect what God has given if it divorces itself from a relationship with God? How can you protect something while at the same time severing ties with it? You cannot! The concept of "separation of church and state" literally prevents Government from effectively performing its stated duty. Although more people still believe in God than not, we are now being governed by an institution that has separated itself from God, using His power to do so. This is shown in picture #16.

"Separation of church & state" separates us from God

Picture #16

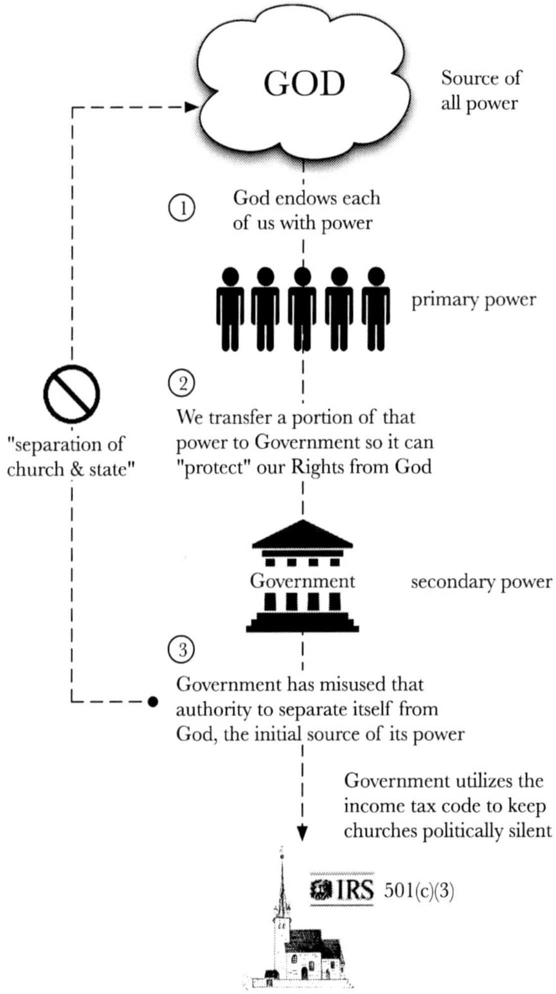

GOD — Source of all power

① God endows each of us with power

primary power

② We transfer a portion of that power to Government so it can "protect" our Rights from God

"separation of church & state"

Government — secondary power

③ Government has misused that authority to separate itself from God, the initial source of its power

Government utilizes the income tax code to keep churches politically silent

IRS 501(c)(3)

88

This diagrams states the following:

- God, who is the source of all power, has given each of us power to operate.

- Man has created Government and given it a portion of our power (consent) to protect our Rights from God.

- Government has taken that power (authority) and separated itself from God.

What nerve! Can you see why things are getting worse, instead of better? Man's-government is actually using power that initially came from God to separate itself from God! Government is literally biting the very hand that feeds it.

God's influence on Man's-government

The influence of God was supposed to be one of many methods used to keep Government in check. The Founders understood that Government is a dangerous necessity, but because it has special authority to use potential deadly force upon its citizens, its power needs to be kept in check. The various methods used to do just that included separating government into three branches, establishing the US Constitution, using the consent of the People via the voting process, acknowledging that States have the Right to secede from the Union, the act of nullification and protecting the 2nd Amendment (the Right to bear arms). However, the greatest and most important method of keeping the institution of Government in check was its accountability to God - that those in governing positions would have to answer to God on Judgment day regarding their just or unjust government of others. This very reason is why Government should not "officially" separate itself from God. By doing so, its accountability to God becomes nonexistent and absent in the eyes of the People.

When you separate a nation from God, you move away from God-rule towards Man-rule. As the influence of God is decreased in a society, Government's allegiance is increased. The ideology of EVERY political party is based upon this concept. Each political party is defined by how many "parts of God" and how many "parts of Government" it is made up of. This is why Christians can't be Democrats. It is because the Democrat Party has a greater mix of Man's-government than it does of God's-government. This does not mean that the Party does not believe in God. It means that their policies lean more towards using the methods of Man, rather than God, for solutions. This is not initially apparent, because the Democrat Party promotes itself in a way that seems to better reflect what we know about God (i.e. equality, fairness, helping the poor). Yet, you cannot expand the authority of Government (force) without losing God (freedom) in the process. This is the fallacy of mankind in general. Although the Republican Party is far from perfect, it believes in a lesser amount of Man's-government, which naturally increases God's-government in society.

The Framers' intent

The distinctions between the 1st Amendment, "separation of church and state" and God's influence on Government are illustrated in picture #17.

Picture #17

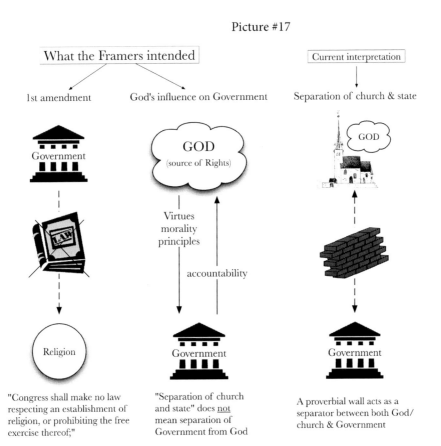

As you can see, the 1st Amendment, God's influence on Government and "separation of church and state" are not one in the same. As a nation, we have been so dumbed down in our understanding of government that we are actually being used as pawns in assisting with this separation. We have bought into the political correctness of "equality" so much so that we have given atheists equal Government leverage, all in the name of not "offending" anyone. We have relied upon politicians, lawyers, judges and so-called "Constitutional scholars" to convince us that God and Government should divorce from each other. Nonsense! How can you expect to receive a "moral and just" Government that has terminated its relationship with God, who is the "source" of morality, accountability and virtues? A Government not accountable and firmly rooted in God will surely become despotic, ruling with absolute power over the People. The following quote warns us of this:

"Man will ultimately be governed by God or by tyrants."
~ Benjamin Franklin

Takeaways:

- The Declaration of Independence "binds" Government to God.

- Neither "separation" nor "church" appear in our Constitution.

- The 1st Amendment prevents the federal Congress from creating a Government theocracy, in which those in power rule by a particular religious belief.

- The 1st Amendment placed limits on the Federal Congress, not churches nor the People.

- Government cannot protect things of God if it has severed ties with Him.

- "Separation of church and state" erects a wall in-between freedom (God) and force (Government).

- God represents all things good; separating from God is separating from His goodness.

It makes no sense that the Founders would create a system of government that was founded upon a belief in a Creator and God-given Rights, only to put a crack in that foundation with the concept of "separation of church and state." When Government separates itself from God, it is left only to its vices. It literally cuts itself off from the healing of God's virtues. Government cannot detach itself from God and expect to operate with success. It is a tragedy to see our Republic go from "one nation under God" towards a nation absent of God.

Keep in mind that Congress does not have to pass laws to fundamentally change the underlying foundation of our nation. All someone has to do is convince enough people and those in Congress to publicly separate themselves and the rest of Government from God. Once the nation has been separated from its foundational "Rock," it will be ruled under the iron fist of Men. Throughout history, we have witnessed the results of what happens when ungodly Men rule over all others.

"Keep your friends close and your enemies closer" ~ Proverb

Suggested translation for Government - "Keep the People close to God, but keep the institution which governs over them even closer."

CHAPTER 12

THE ROAD TO HELL

"The road to hell is paved with good intentions" ~ *Proverb*

*"Good intentions will always be pleaded for every assumption
of authority. It is hardly too strong to say that the Constitution was made to guard the people against the dangers of good
intentions. There are men in all ages who mean to govern well,
but they mean to govern. They promise to be good masters, but
they mean to be masters."~ Daniel Webster*

The "Good Intention" Enemy

One of the greatest enemies of our Rights is the concept of Government "good intentions." Politicians have been and will continue to sell us on their "good intentions" as a way to increase their power and reach. It is one of their greatest political tools. Question - why do we continue to get suckered into their trap time and time again? I suspect that deep down inside, we truly want to believe that the outcome will be good, as intended. Because of such naivety, we continue to hand more authority and responsibility over to the Government, as if they actually know what is best for mankind. As Christians, we already know that Man cannot be the savior of others, regardless of the good intention. Good results come from your own doings, not those of the politician. The best thing they can do is move out of the way.

The sell of "good intentions" also comes up when the politician decides he or she wants to address or dictate morality (God's morality). Because most of us want a moral society, we often enlist the politician with the responsibility of being "Mr. & Mrs. Morality." In doing so, a "sin" tax is sure to follow. A sin tax is a tax levied upon certain "so-called" immoral products, such as cigarettes, alcohol, fatty foods, soft drinks and certain services, such as strip clubs and gambling. Under the guise of "good intentions," the politician will attempt to financially tax you out of your sinful and immoral behaviors, thus somehow forcing you towards morality. Now, think about it - if there were a sin tax for every man-made vice, we'd all be broke! It is not the role of Government to tax you out of your vices and into morality. The end result is that citizens are taxed more and those in Government become more powerful.

Just because the Government tells us that something is good does not mean it is. God has already given us the tools required to obtain good results (i.e. morality, virtues, commandments, principles, high conscience). They all can be found in your "God-basket." When applied, they far exceed anything Government can do.

Forced intentions are the enemy of God's blessings

When you utilize Government to enact good intentions, you are actually doing an injustice to God. To understand why, we need to examine what happens during the process:

- Like everything else the Government gets involved with, it enforces its policies via laws. Laws always limit the individual and are enforced by guns. Barring specific political connections, you do not have the option of opting out of laws.

- Since force is used, God is not present and therefore cannot be used to justify the act.

- The more Government force that is used, the more distant God and the things of God become. Therefore, such things as Rights, freedom, morality and love are also sacrificed in the process.

Simply, when you increase Man's-government, you conversely decrease God's-government. Considering that all things that are good come from God, you also decrease such things from society, such as independence, abundance, morality, virtues and love. You cannot push God out of society and expect the things of God to remain.

So, although it may appear that you are endorsing what appears to be good, once it channels through Government, God is removed from the process. This is shown in picture #18.

Picture #18

The results of forced "good intentions"

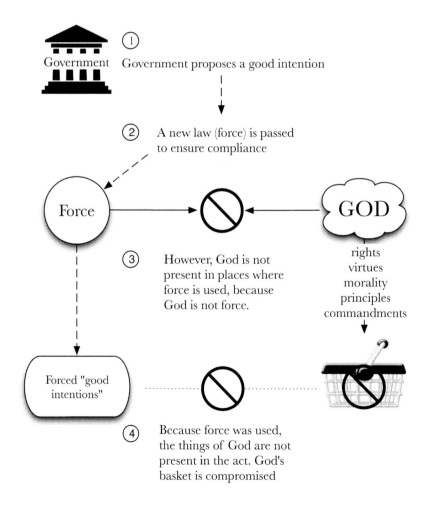

Takeaways:

- Once a "good intention" is forced, it is no longer "good."

- Government-forced "good intentions" negates Rights, freedom and property.

- With each, new good intention, Man-rule increases over God-rule.

- Government's role is to protect our God-given Rights, not protect us from ourselves.

Sometimes it is the dislike and disdain of those things and people that are not "Christ-like" that allows many Christians to justify using Man's-government to address such things. Yet, every time the Government gets into the business of "good intentions," someone always loses their Rights in the process. This is because in order to do something good for all, someone or something must be sacrificed during the process. As Christians, we should be in the business of protecting what God has given, not lose it to the presumptions of Man's "good intentions." Through the propaganda of "good intentions," Government has dictated our healthcare, diet, finances, education and the rearing of our children. To make matters worse, it has robbed us of our individuality and even the God-given Right to our own emotions. Anyone who opposes is publicly ridiculed in an effort to silence them. All along, the presence of God, who is the essence of goodness, is nowhere to be found.

Question - how can "good intentions" be derived from the force of Government?

It cannot! Forced "good intentions" creates the oxymoron of "good force." Basically, the Government is forces good upon us. Actually, it sounds more like "force-feeding," something you do with children. I ask you, are we children of God or Government?

Because of its noble beliefs, the Democrat Party tends to impose more "good intentions" policies more often than not. Although their hearts may be in the right place, the Democrat Party is somewhat delusional in thinking that

Government-forced "good intentions" are actually "good." As Christians, we know that the immoralities of Man are better addressed through the ways of God, not through Government's laws and taxes. This is why Christians can't be Democrats.

> *"Hi, I'm from the government, and I'm here to help."*
> *~ Source unknown*

CHAPTER 13

THE TEN "DEMANDMENTS"

"I think Democrats keep the commandments of the Lord more."
~ Lincoln Davis

Demandment - a forced commandment (origin unknown)

Imagine what type of world we would have if God had decided to issue the Ten "Demandments," rather than the Ten Commandments. Not only would we be forced to comply with every "demandment" issued by God, we would have the additional responsibility of demanding God's demandments upon others (believers and non-believers alike). Such a responsibility would give us the justification to use force throughout the world, ensuring that all followed God's demands. Such responsibility would pit us against our neighbors, coworkers, family members and other religious factions. The world would become so full of force that it could no longer be recognized as being of God. Well, fortunately God did "not" issue the Ten Demandments, yet some Christians behave as if He had. They insist that everyone follow God's commandments as if they were demands. They carry that belief directly into the voting booth - voting for that politician who campaigned on seeing those "demandments" through. These Christians conveniently use Government as a way to force God's commandments upon all others. These "Christians" defend themselves by hiding behind the notion that it is the will of God. These Christians have conveniently made commands and demands synonymous terms. Are you such a Christian? Have you delegated God's commandments and your Christian responsibilities over to Man's-Government out of convenience and as a matter of expediency?

So, why is it that God issued the "Ten Commandments" instead of the "Ten Demandments?" To answer this question, we must first review what we know about God and then define the difference between a command and a demand.

God is LOVE

God is a loving God. God is the ultimate love; therefore God is the ultimate freedom. If you truly love someone, you must eventually give him or her individual freedom. God truly loves us and therefore has given us individual free will. He has given us the free will to believe in Him or not. He has given us the free will of self-determination. He has even given us the free will to engage in virtues (moral behavior) as well as in vices (immoral behavior). In order for us to love God the way He desires, we must first have the freedom to accept or reject Him. In other words, we must have the complete freedom to turn away from God and/or return to Him. It is at the point that we "freely" return to God that true, mutual and unconditional love is established. True love cannot be established out of force or duress. Yes, God is love.

Commands and Demands

Simply defined, a Command is an order; a Demand is a forced order. When it comes to Commands and Demands, the former represents freedom and the latter dictates force. Although they both may have consequences if not followed, you have the freedom not to follow a Command, but you are forced to follow a Demand.

Question - If there are consequences for not following a command or a demand, then why does the difference between the two even matter? The consequence is still there regardless.

Answer - If both commands and demands could be equally enforced, then individual freedom would be compromised. Anyone could force you to follow their commands and demands. You could not freely walk away from either. You would be forced to comply. If someone commanded you to do something unethical, you would have no choice but to comply. This is not freedom - it is force. God offers us Freedom, even if we are aware of the consequences. It is because God is LOVE that we are able to choose whether or not to comply with His commandments.

100

When you utilize Government to broker the transfer between God's commandments to the People, it becomes the middleman between the People and God, which contradicts the "Freedom formula" - G-m=F (God - man = Freedom). Picture #19 illustrates this point.

Picture #19

God's commands get converted into Man's demands

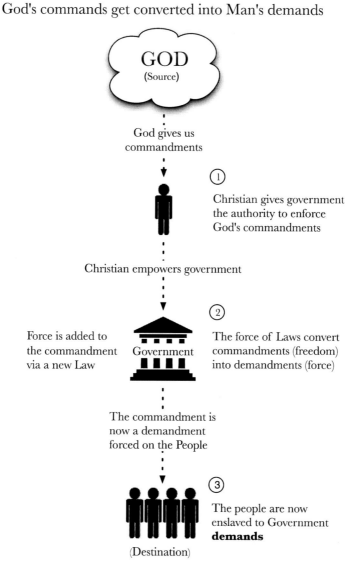

(Destination)

To align ourselves more with Christ, we must ensure that God's commandments are allowed to flow down to ALL people, not just some. His commandments must remain unaltered by mankind in the process. However, when Government enters into the process, it becomes broken. The moment we empower Man's-government with the responsibility of enforcing God's commandments, we effectively convert God's commands into Man's demands.

Here is the formula for converting a command into a demand:

C+F=D (Command + Force = Demand)

Since Government operates out of force, it can also be written as:

C+G=D (Command + Government = Demand)

It is hypocritical of Christians to "demand commands," especially considering that God does not "demand commands" of us. The same free will that God has allowed for you must also be allowed for others. Each time you use force to make others comply with a commandment, you are increasing Man-rule over God-rule. This is because you have taken something that started off being from God and ended up under the control of Man. The commandment started off as one thing and ended up being another. Once you add force, it can no longer be claimed as being from God. Why do we, as Christians, demand that others follow God's commandments? Why do we, as Christians, see a need to force God's commandments upon others, although He does not force them upon us? What if they do not believe in God? Should they still be forced to comply with His commandments? Do we now know better than God on what is best for our fellow man? We have taken the commandments of the Master, added force and converted them into demandments for our masters in Washington. Through our noble intentions, we have given Government the responsibility, justification and the power to create innumerable laws to dictate morality on both the "sinner" and Christian alike. We have become pawns in the battle of Man's-rule and God's-rule.

We've been duped!

The Democrat Party campaigns on the platform of equality, fairness, wanting to do the "right thing," protecting the "little guy" or helping those that are "less fortunate." The Christian voter, who also wants equality, fairness, to do the right thing, help protect the little guy and help the less fortunate, identifies with these deeds as the noble, Christian thing to do. This builds rapport between the Christian, the politician and the political party. They both now share common "Christian" ground, based on God's commandments. The Christian aligns themselves with the Democrat Party and then empowers the politician with the authority to see God's commandments through, not knowing they have just added force to the mix. However, what the politician sells us and what they tell us are hardly the same. They hide behind the methods. They do not openly share that they must use discrimination (a vice) as a way to accomplish "God's will." They especially mask the power transfer from the People to Government. They do not tell us that they must use the force to do the work of the Lord.

Again, you cannot take a commandment from God, add the force of Man and still claim that it is of God. This is called conversion. It is illegal under the laws of Man and unjust under the laws of God. Too many people justify using Government's force as a way to expedite the process of God's commandments. Although the process may be slow at times, we must be patient (one of God's virtues). Adding the force of man to speed of the ways and will of God sounds ridiculous if spoken aloud, yet this has been the mind set of some. Plus, putting this responsibility upon the shoulders of Man's-government removes personal accountability - the "Government" has no physical face (non-tangible). It has no true identity, therefore cannot be singled-out for blame - "out of sight out of mind." Using Government to force God's commandments on other citizens opens the floodgates for other religious and non-religious groups to follow suit. It eventually becomes a race of which religious group can build up its power base in Washington. Each must now use the tactics of lobbying, corruption, extortion and money to entice politicians to advance their cause. The politician, all the while, becomes a highly paid and all-powerful benefactor in the process. In the end, the religious group with the most influence gets the opportunity to apply its faith values upon others. God's commands must remain wholly intact from their source (God) to their destination (the individual). They should be untouched and unaltered by human hands and immediately rejected the very moment they are manipulated with force.

"Necessity is the plea for every infringement of human freedom.
It is argument of tyrants. It is the creed of slaves."
~ William Pitt

Takeaways:

- A Command is an order that you can freely choose to follow or not.

- A Demand is an order that you are forced to follow.

- God issues Commands; Man issues Demands.

- God's Commandments + Government = Demandments (C+G=D).

- God's Commandments that have been converted into demandments can no longer be claimed as being from God.

We cannot effectively follow God's commandments of us while at the same time living under Government's demands on us. They are opposing foes on a sliding scale. To demand a command is a contradiction. Like other principles within this book, the two cannot operate in the very same space at the very same time. We should encourage others to follow God's commands, not seek to enslave them by demanding that they do. If at any time in the future God wishes to force us to follow His commandments, He will not need the help of Man. Although God commands certain things of us, He does not accomplish it by using force - neither should we.

THE FORCE IS "NOT" THE SOURCE

CHAPTER 14

TAKE ME TO YOUR LEADER!

"You do not lead by hitting people over the head — that's assault, not leadership." ~ *Dwight D. Eisenhower*

-- Leader - a person followed by others

Man's-government cannot lead you

Turn on the television or radio any given day and you will most likely hear someone refer to those in Government as leaders. This term has been used so frequently to describe Government officials that we have become conditioned into believing it. When mentioned, the "leadership" title is never challenged, but not because those hearing it take offense; it is because they actually agree! However, not only is it generally impossible for Government officials to be leaders, it is a very dangerous notion that must be corrected immediately. The fate of our nation relies upon it. Somewhere along the way, we have watered down our understanding of what defines a leader. Over time, we have both redefined and cheapened its definition and qualifications. A leader used to represent someone who had certain characteristics, such as being knowledgeable, inspirational and trustworthy. We now equate the leader as the person who has the most power, perceived or not. Leader and power have become synonymous and complimenting terms. This is most unfortunate. By deeming those within Government as leaders, we have subconsciously place ourselves in an inferior position to them. Because of the perceived inferiority, there is also a mental shift of power, from the People to Government. Calling those in Government "leaders" is one of the greatest cop-outs by citizens. Empowering Government with the leadership title allows society to conveniently displace its challenges and burdens upon the shoulders of politicians. It gives us a convenient escape route from personal responsibility and accountability, not to mention the justification to complain when they fail - which they surely will. Those "leaders" eventually become fall guys; public punching bags for the American people, who will raise torches and pitchforks demanding new fall guys. Unfortunately, we no longer elect representatives with the duty of protecting our unalienable Rights. We currently use the election cycle as a way to deflect and shift our personal burdens and responsibilities to the next political fall guy, previously aware that man cannot save man. Shame on the People!

Regardless of a person's characteristics, accomplishments and/or title, there is only one thing that qualifies them as a leader - that you "freely" and "willingly" choose to follow them. If you are being forced to follow, then you are not being led - you are being forcefully pushed. There are some very good leaders and there are some really bad ones. Whether they are good or bad leaders does not matter one bit. If you are willingly following them, then they are leading. The choice of who leads you is yours and yours alone. Absolutely no one can pick a leader for you, nor can you pick a leader for someone else. This concept applies to Government representatives, CEOs, managers, captains of sporting teams, school principles, pastors and even parents. As a matter of fact, this concept applies to any organization in which leaders are elected or assigned. For clarity, this applies to personal leadership - not "leading" in the sense of being ahead of the competition. For example, a particular company may be leading its industry in sales and or innovation. However, that does not mean that the CEO of that company is the leader by virtue of having the title. Please be careful not to automatically link titles to the concept of leadership. You will find yourself seeking out those with certain titles, believing there are leadership qualities lurking nearby.

The reason that those within Government, as an institution, cannot be leaders is because Government operates out of force, which is a direct contradiction to the primary qualification of leadership - the "freedom" to follow. It is therefore disqualified to lead by proxy. This does not mean that particular individuals within Government cannot be an inspiration and/or offer personal leadership to others. It just means that they should not automatically be viewed as leaders just because they have a position in Government or because someone called them one. Some people in Government defend their "leadership" title by stating it was secured by the People's popular vote (majority rule). However, as previously stated, no one can choose a leader for anyone else. America is a Republic, not a "Democracy" of majority rule. Therefore, the majority cannot choose leaders for the minority, regardless if the term "leader" or "president" is the position that is being voted upon. Considering that the losing minority voted for someone else initially, the elected "leader" was obviously not their first choice for leadership. Thus, the minority really conceded in the election process. In other words, if there is no doubt on who the leader should be, then why are you even voting? The newly elected leader is no more a "leader" to the losing minority voters now than he/she was before the vote. To the losing minority, he or she is just now viewed as "the person in charge."

Contrary to popular belief, the president is not the leader of the United States, nor the leader or executive over the whole Federal government. Nowhere within the US Constitution is it implied that the role of the president is to lead or govern over all of Government and/or the nation. Recall, that the president is a member of the executive branch of government, not the legislative or judicial branches. We have three, separate branches at the Federal level to prevent any one person from having too much power. Although the president is often introduced as "Commander in Chief," two words that imply leadership, a quick examination of the Constitution will clarify the title to be "Commander in Chief of the Army and Navy ..." If it were intended that the president be the leader of all Government and/or the nation, then the Founding Fathers might as well have kept King George III onboard in 1776. Our nation was centralized under God, not the president. Each individual was to lead him or herself under the guidance of God - not one Man.

Not only are those in Government not our leaders, we should not want them to be. This is because it is in our best interest to keep Government in a position of servitude, not leadership. You cannot lead while at the same time being led. Recall, the origin of the word "govern" means "to steer." If placed in a superior position above the People, combined with the authority to use deadly force to meet its objective, the People would effectively be under a dictatorship. We would become servants to our own secondary power! Secondary power should never become the master or leader over its primary power source. To keep Government inferior and accountable to the People, the Declaration of Independence stated that Government must have consent of the People. Again, this implies that we delegate and give consent to Government, not them delegating and giving consent to us. Also, do not fall into the belief that global Government officials are "world leaders." We are not subjects of a collective world power. All of Man's-government, domestic or international, operates out of force! Whenever these global officials meet, their intentions may be global economic solutions and peace, but their discussed methods are based on some form of force. How can you lead yourself while at the same time being forced to follow? If we continue to look at those in Government as leaders, then we will most likely start looking towards them to lead, while we, the People, follow like sheep (a.k.a. "sheeple").

Our nation has morphed from individual leadership under the guidance of God to the forced-collective under the rule of Man. In order to re-position the nation under God and slow the rise of Man-rule, we must immediately stop referring those in Government as our leaders. The next time you cast your vote, ensure that you are electing someone who will represent you, not lead you. Likewise, children are being indoctrinated into believing that those in Government are their leaders, later carrying this mind-set into the voting booth. From a very young age, they are being taught that Man's-government leads and that they should follow like good, little citizens rather than to lead themselves. To qualify for your vote, politicians should, at the minimum, understand their primary duty - to protect the God-given rights of each individual, regardless of ethnicity, race, sexual preference, gender, age, etc. If they do not understand this basic job function, then he or she is positioning themselves to be a soldier on the side of Man's-government. We are not losing the battle between Man versus God because we do not understand the difference between Man and God. We are losing the battle because we do not understand how to protect those things which are of God from the control of Man. By the way, God did not send politicians to lead you out of bondage. The difference between Man's-government and Moses is that those who freely followed Moses could have opted out at any time. Try opting out of Government "leadership."

Takeaways:

- A leader is someone that you are willing to follow, not someone you are forced to follow.

- No one can pick a leader for you, nor you for them.

- Powerful and leader are not mutually-inclusive terms.

- Those within Government (secondary power) are not our leaders, superiors, nor our peers; they are servants of the People.

The Framers of the Constitution understood that those in Government are servants (inferior) to the People. Current-day society speaks of those within Government as our leaders (superior). This fundamental shift in thinking is why America is on the decline. Our servants have become our masters.

Thought - If aliens from space were to come into your community, organization or place of employment, and demand that they'd be taken to the leader, would everyone take them to see the same person?

CHAPTER 15

I'VE COME TO "BLESS" YOU

"Every step we take towards making the State our Caretaker
of our lives, by that much we move toward making the
State our Master." ~ Dwight D. Eisenhower

Contrary to what many people believe, Government cannot "bless" you. This is because blessings come from God, not Government. Also, because God represents freedom, He does not channel your blessing through Government, which is force. Recall that the two cannot occupy the very same space at the very same time. Therefore, God's blessings cannot flow through a pipeline filled with force. It would get blocked along the way. Government has no resources of its own, therefore it cannot "bless" its citizens with anything (i.e. jobs, entitlements, money). Any attempt to do so requires that Government intercept the God-given blessings of others. In order for the Democrat Party to fulfill its ideological goals such as entitlement programs (i.e. housing, healthcare, food programs), it must change Government's role of protecting personal property Rights to confiscating it. This is why Christians can't be Democrats. God has given us the Right to obtain personal property and has commanded us not to steal from others nor covet our neighbor's possessions. Because stealing is not a method of God, the act of providing entitlements is absent of His blessings, and therefore done in vain. The very moment you utilize Government to do the work of Christ (the very work that you should be doing yourself), you contradict and compromise everything that Christ stood for. Besides, God does not bless the community that openly accepts "stolen goods" from Government. Such communities actually suffer long-term consequences by doing so. They stay in perpetual poverty because God does not condone stealing. Rather than getting better, the community actually declines. This is because each time it accepts "stolen goods (i.e. blessings)" from Government, it becomes more dependent upon Government and thus enslaved to it. Recall that Government is a secondary power. Therefore, dependent communities, which once held primary power, eventually become enslaved to their secondary power. This power swap is an abomination in nature. This is why communities that operate in this manner will never come up from and out of financial or mental poverty. The methods used to address their situations are done with the force of Man, rather than the love of God and the methods of Christ. Simply, God does not bless the thief, nor does He operate in places where force was invited in. When you give consent for Government to rob your fellow citizens for the sake of your own or someone else's benefit, you are an accomplice to the act of thievery. Just like the community that accepts the stolen goods, you will also suffer the consequences. When you condone Government stealing, you are contributing not only to the enslavement of communities, but also to the destruction of our nation - the very nation built upon the principles of God.

> *"When the people find that they can vote themselves*
> *money, that will herald the end of the republic."*
> *~ Benjamin Franklin*

When you vote other people's money, you are voting to remove their God-given Rights to property ownership. Once you go down that slippery slope it is only a matter of time before your property becomes due! As Christians, we should be sharing our God-given blessings with others. Yet, how can we share our blessing if Government hijacks them en route? Therefore, it is important that we do not empower government with too much responsibility, because the mighty wage is our power and money. The way to truly help people and communities can be found in God's virtue of "charity," not Government aid.

Charity vs. Government Aid

Charity is based on the virtue of compassion. Compassion is sympathetically or empathetically sharing resources with others who may be suffering or experiencing a misfortune. God wants us to be compassionate. It is one of His many virtues. Compassion allows us to freely share our blessings with others. The key here is "freely." If you were forced to share your blessing with others, then your personal act of kindness, compassion, sympathy or empathy are no

114

longer part of the act of giving. God blesses the compassionate person because they are being virtuous. However, once Government (force) enters the picture, the act can no longer be considered compassionate, nor is it blessed by God, as God does not bless a forceful or immoral act.

During times of catastrophe, both domestically and internationally, we have all seen or heard various presidents proclaim how compassionate the United States is, followed by their vow to offer up millions in so-called "Government aid" to help in the relief. Well, there is something extremely misleading and incorrect in that statement. First, it gives the impression that Americans have "collectively" agreed to willingly give up those millions or billions. However, this is quite the opposite of what happens. Anytime a president makes this pledge, understand that you are going to be forced to contribute. You do not have the option of opting out. Second, there is no such thing as a "compassionate Government." The term is an oxymoron. Compassion is a virtue that inspires the act of charity - "freely" sharing your God-given blessings with others. On the contrary, if you forcefully take possessions from one neighbor to help out other neighbor, that is not charity - that is stealing. Your intent may have been good, but the way you went about it was wrong.

The Act of Giving

To illustrate the difference between Charity and Government Aid, let's compare the approach of Peter, the politician and Nancy, the noble neighbor. Both Peter and Nancy want to help others in their local community and they have decided to use their respective positions to do so:

Nancy, the noble neighbor, chooses to freely share some of her own blessings with others within the community. Peter, the politician, decides to submit or support legislation that requires taxing a specific group of people (discrimination), in order to collect enough money to help the community. In other words, Peter wants to give from the pockets of others, rather than his own. Keep in mind that since legislation has been passed, Peter can now rely upon the force of Government to collect the money he intends to use for the community. Eventually, using the methods of both Nancy and Peter, the community was financially helped, but through entirely different methods, which produced extremely different results:

Nancy's way followed the methods of Christ. Through her noble act of compassion, the community retained its dignity and remained non-obligated to Nancy.

Peter, on the other hand, used the force of Government. Because a law was passed to implement the "compassion," both the community and those directly affected by the law become enslaved to Peter. The community becomes indentured (enticed) slaves. That's to say, to ensure that they always receive the "blessings" of Peter (the politician), they necessarily must vote for him or his political party. Those individuals who succumbed under the new tax law become chattel (forced) slaves; they are now forced by the Government to stay in compliance with the new law of "giving." Now, considering both sides are now enslaved to Government, they both lose a certain amount of independence and power; that same power needed to take risks and dig themselves out of any situation that may arise in the future. However, by the time the next election cycle comes around, the powerless community has yet to recover. Thus, Peter the politician can make his political pitch on how he can save the day once again. Because people are self-preserving, they embrace the idea of being enslaved for another political term and the cycle continues.

Unfortunately, too many Americans view both Nancy's and Peter's acts as being compassionate. However, Peter is seen more as a "savior," considering his methods contributed more physical dollars into the community than Nancy's, thus securing him another political term. Our Constitutional-Republic was founded upon the belief that God endowed the individual and the role of the "Peters" in Government is to protect those endowments. However, Government cannot protect your endowments from God if those endowments have been confiscated from you prior. In other words, the Government cannot both play God and protect your Rights from God at the same time. It's one or the other. The "Peters" in Government have intercepted our blessings from God, redistributed them to others, and taken credit for saving the day!

Pictures #20 and #21 illustrate the difference between God's charity and Government aid. Notice how the Man's-government forcefully injects itself as a middleman in-between the People and God's intended blessings. This conflicts with the Freedom formula: God minus government equals freedom (G-g=F).

How Charity works

Picture #20

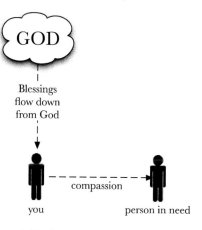

1. Blessings flow down from God to you

2. Out of compassion, you "freely" share your God-given blessings with others

   Compassion is one of God's virtues; you are not forced to give

Picture #21

How Government Aid works

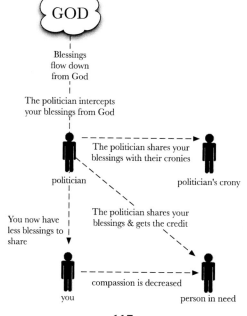

117

Takeaways:

- Charity is derived from compassion; Government aid is derived via force.

- God did not send politicians to "bless you." He is capable on His own.

- You cannot share your blessings if you are being robbed of them.

- God does not bless a thief nor those who openly accept "stolen" blessings.

- Government is supposed to protect God's blessings, not intercept and redistribute them.

- Entitlements are the enemy of Rights.

- Be more compassionate and demand that Government get out the "charity" business.

A big part of the Democrat platform and why so many Christians possibly vote Democrat is because of the perception that the party assists in helping those in need. However, it has always been shown that the "needy-minded" stay in need. The politician can always be assured of their vote. Be assured that God would absolutely want us to help others, but not under duress at the threat of a Government gun. As Christians, we must help wean individuals off of Government dependency programs by replacing them with charitable giving. This will be challenging though, as too many people have become too dependent on Man. Also, because humans are self-preserving, this will be more challenging for those without jobs. Yet, we must remain faithful that God's way will offer independence and abundance, as He is the source for both when done under His methods. We must also seek to reduce overall Government influence over communities. To pray to God for blessings, but to get them delivered by Government has an amazing ability to shift a person's allegiance over time. Prayer goes up to God, yet Government delivers the blessings. After awhile, just like a trained lab rat, people start showing up at the very spot where they are expecting a payout. Where people used to show up at churches to receive charity; they now show up at government offices. Where we used to live to serve the "Master," we now serve the politicians in Washington in order to live. Dependency has become the "new" independence. Now that government has a 501(c)(3) tax-exempt hold over churches, the "new" pastor is now the politician, preaching the sermon of security, provisions and entitlements in the name of God. They have moved the proverbial pulpit from the private sector (non-government) to the public sector (Government), dragging dependency along the way, with enslavement close behind. If the very essence of your livelihood (i.e. food, housing or healthcare) is dependent upon decisions made in Congress, then you have already become enslaved to the system of Man's-government. Go find and reclaim the items in you God basket.

Question - are you currently a "Christian" enabler, helping to enslave God's people by authorizing Man's-government to be the provider of their needs?

> *"...If 'Thou shalt not covet,' and 'Thou shalt not steal,' were*
> *not commandments of Heaven, they must be made inviolable*
> *precepts in every society, before it can be civilized or made free."*
> *~ John Adams*

CHAPTER 16

THE DONKEY AND THE ELEPHANT

"It's not that Republicans do Man's-government better than the
Democrats; they just do a little less of it."
~ Michael D. Thomas

No, Christians absolutely cannot be Democrats, but nor should they strive to be Republicans either. This is because the Republican Party is not the final stop on the Christian's political journey. The Republican Party only serves as a temporary resting place for those Christian exiting the Democrat Party. From there, we should continue towards the political-right, back under the government of God. Because of the political influence of both parties, chances are that most our politicians will likely come from either of the two parties for some time to come. Therefore, the goal is to make a political migration from one major political party to the other, only as a way to change political policy. Again, this migration is only temporary. The Republican Party is not "home" to the Christian voter no more than the Democrat Party is. However, it is one step closer to the political-right. Like all other political groups, the Republican Party is not without its faults and is far from perfect. It is obvious that both parties have gone beyond their government duties. Voting republican doesn't imply that you are a more informed voter or a better Christian. Many of the reasons why some people vote republican are the very same reasons that others vote democrat. It could be because of how your parents voted; it could be some pre-conceived political beliefs; it could be that you are tired of the failures of the "other" party. As a matter of speaking, there are politicians within the Republican Party who do not understand the Republican ideology, or the role of government or where Rights come from. However, when it comes to your

Christian vote, it is your obligation to make an educated decision, based on your newfound understanding of God's-government, Man's-government and your Christian faith. Although political parties will come and go, the principles in God's nature and the methods of Christ will remain eternal and unchanged. Therefore, the philosophies and theories within this book will always remain relevant and aligned with Christian beliefs - do you vote for God's-government or Man-government?

Democrats and Republicans

Neither Democrats nor Republicans dispute the various challenges America is currently facing. Their disagreement revolves around whose methods should be used to solve them - God's way or Man's way. It may seem obvious that we would want to use God's way of fixing our problems, yet this is not necessarily the case or so obvious to most people. This is because it is hard to distinguish between God's way and Man's way when viewing things through a "political" lens. As discussed in previous chapters, it is not about what is being promoted, but rather "how" it is being accomplished. For example, anybody can call himself or herself a Christian, but what do their "actions" reveal about who they really are? To proclaim something, but purposely contradict that claim is hypocrisy. Although the Republican Party could use a serious public relations makeover, its policies actually align more with God's principles in nature than the Democrat's, whether the Republican Party is aware of it or not. This is to say, the Democrat Party promotes what Christ would want and the Republican Party more aligned with how Christ would go about accomplishing it, based on principles in nature.

Before comparing how the Democrat and Republican policies align with God, it is important to "mentally" separate the person (the politician) from the machine (their respective political party). In other words, try not to define the ideology or temperament of the party, as a whole, based on the actions of individual politicians. It is the job of the politician to woo you with their rhetoric and charisma. Therefore, try to separate this from the principles for which the party actually stands for. Without doing so, the ideologies of the two parties get really cloudy. This is because it is human nature to associate the outcome of something with a particular person. For example, most people blindly give credit to the president when times are good and discredit the president when times are bad. They do not take in account that it takes several years for political policies to run their course. Nor do they take into account that the Constitution limits the authority of the president via enumerated powers (a list of what the federal government can do, rather than not do). Too many people give the president "virtual" power and place the office of the Presidency upon the proverbial pedestal. We defer to the president to speak on his perspective of every possible media event. This is a clear sign that America believes that the president is our leader. This is inferior thinking. Until we better understand the very Government that governs over us, we will continue to be disappointed in our Government. Just as no one person encompasses and defines an entire religion, no one person represents and defines a nation or political party. This is why it is best to vote the principles of a particular party, rather than vote the person. The person, given enough time, will always fail you. For example, if the "person in charge" at your place of worship failed in their religious duties, do you switch religions? Most likely the answer is "no." This is because that person does not define that religion or your religious conviction. However, for some reason, we do not apply that same logic to politics. If a president failed in their duty, we tend to dismiss the whole ideology of the party they represented, even if the ideology is fundamentally sound in its principles. Just as you have your convictions of your religion, you should remain steadfast to those principles that make sense, even if the person elected to execute upon those principles failed. The fact remains that "Man" will always fail you eventually, so stay true to your beliefs and convictions.

In reviewing the end result of their policies, a major difference between the Republicans and Democrats is that the Republicans believe it is not the role of Government to take care of its citizens, but to protect their unalienable Rights from God. The Democrats believe it is okay for Government to help provide for its citizens, even if it is at the expense of others. Republican policies tend to have government serving the People, while Democrat policies tend to have the People serving the demands of Government. It would be too time consuming to compare all of established and/or proposed policies between the two parties and beyond the scope of this book to do so. Not only that, it is not really necessary to dive into the policy details. Simply, when reviewing the policies of the two parties, the following litmus test will tell you if the policy lines up with God's-government or Man's-government.

Democrat and Republican websites:

Democrat Party - www.democrats.org
Republican Party - www.gop.org

If the policy seeks to "protect" the Rights of "all" citizens, then it aligns more with God's-government. Such policies protect what God has given us.

If the policy seeks to "provide" citizens "Government-imposed" Rights, equality, fairness or entitlements, then it aligns more with Man's-government. Such policies require that the Rights of others are compromised or removed to provide a privilege.

Democrats

Before going forward, let us be very clear - the Democrat Party is not "anti-God." To the contrary, the Democrat Party and its supporters are made up of wonderful people of all type of backgrounds, who, for the most part, share in the same noble beliefs of helping others and doing what they believe is right, fair, equal and just. The reasons why Christians cannot be Democrats has little to do with the people within the Democrat Party, but more to do with the party's huge reliance upon Man's-government to achieve its goals. Attempting to be the "provider of Man" is a huge task that takes an enormous amount of resources and authority. In other words, the noble beliefs of the Democrats are "Christ-inspired," but "Government-acquired." Though such policies promote "Christ-like" ways, they use the force of Government to accomplish them. As previously mentioned, Christ is love, not force; therefore, to use force in the name of Christ or God is hypocrisy. God wants our noble efforts to be "Christ-inspired" and "Christian-acquired." Each time a challenging situation arises in your personal life, you have the option of either utilizing God's way to address it or go it alone utilizing your way (also known as Man's-way). Because of our urgency and desperation to get through the problem, we tend to discard God's-way, as a matter of quick convenience. This is the same route when we look towards Man's-government to address the issues within society. We ignore God's virtue of patience, replacing it with "forced" convenience. Although the Democrat Party promotes itself as being more God-centric in its beliefs, its methods to achieve those beliefs are all Man-centric. What they promote and how they promote it are in conflict.

Many of the Democrat Party policies also tend to start out with a "spirit of distrust." The premise behind this is that mankind, in general, cannot be trusted to do what is right, fair and equal and therefore they must be forced by a law (enslavement) to do the right thing on the "front-end" of a particular action. For example, not "everyone" can be trusted to do the "right" thing, if given the freedom to do so, therefore "no one" will be trusted; thus a law must be created to demand that "all" people do the "right" thing and not be given the freedom to decide for themselves. It makes no difference if the person agrees with whatever the "right" thing is or not. They are forced and enslaved to do so. This is a "spirit of distrust," shown in picture #22.

Picture #22

Democrat policy

The Democrat Party policies tend to have a spirit of distrust.

Not everyone can be trusted to do the "right" things all of the time.

Laws & regulations are used as a way to force & dictate behavior in the name of "good."

Government

In order to keep everyone in compliance, Government's power must increase. God is absent.

Eventually, everyone becomes enslaved to government (Man).

The problem with this type of thinking is that it directly contradicts with the "spirit of God." God has a "spirit of trust" on the front-end of an action. In other words, before we take action on something, He trusts that we will do the "right" thing, although we have the freedom not to do so. Because of this freedom, we are expected to be responsible and accountable in our actions, while following His commandments, principles and virtues. If we find ourselves irresponsible with this freedom, we pay the consequences on the "back-end." Conversely, when you are trying to prevent people from engaging in immoral behaviors or trying to ensure that they are always do the "right" thing, you must remove some of their personal freedoms. After all, if you want to absolutely guarantee a particular outcome of a situation, you have to always have controls present to dictate and enforce actions along the way.

Purposely removing someone's freedoms up-front in order to strongly urge them towards moral behavior is not very God-like at all. It is like saying, "so that you do not use your freedoms for bad things, we will just remove certain freedoms altogether." This is similar to why the Government forcefully confiscates the "social security" portion of your paycheck before you receive it. The Government (secondary power) does not believe that you can be trusted to save for your own retirement if you are allowed to keep it. That is not freedom; especially not God's freedom. Yes, there will be those that choose not to save for their retirement, but everyone's finances should not have to be controlled due to the irresponsibility of some.

Democrat mobocracy (mob-rule)

The current-day Democrat Party believes in the concept of a government democracy of majority rule. Democracy is a term that most everyone has heard of and more people than not believe that the United States is a Democracy form of Government. However, Article 4 section 4 of the US Constitution states that we are a Republican form of Government and that every State in the Union must also have a Republican form of Government. To reiterate, we are not a Democracy.[1] A Democracy of majority-rule is one of the most dangerous types of government systems in existence. This is because individual Rights cannot

1. When most people speak of a Democracy, they are most likely referring to the democratic process, which is not the same as a democracy. A democracy is a government of majority rule by the People. However, the democratic process means "one person; one vote." A democratic vote of a majority does not mean that the majority vote outweighs the minority vote. The beauty in being a Republican form of Government is that the minority is protected from rule of the majority. We use the democratic process to choose our representatives in government.

be protected under a system of majority rule, where 51% of the People can use their political vote to control the other 49%. However, this is the foundation for most Democrat policies, removing the Right of an individual for the benefit of the majority. No civilization can survive when 51% of its citizens can vote away the property of the other 49%. Human beings are self-preserving and will not remain within communities in which the property they labored to obtain is confiscated at will. When Government policies demand redistribution of wealth, fairness and equality, it poses a problem for society. This is because forced fairness, equality and property redistribution requires that someone oversee and referee the process - Government referees don't come cheap! They come at the expense of your property, byway of taxes. Huge mistake! "Tax" is Government code word that means "loss of property." Sometimes this loss is voluntarily (when you purchase something), but more often it's forced (i.e. income tax). Thus, every time taxes are raised, the end result is more of your personal property is lost. Because you had to labor for several hours of your life (which is limited on earth) to obtain it, each time it is taken, that portion of your "life hours" is lost forever. Thus, the more of your property Government takes, the more it owns and controls your labor. Now, this does not mean that we should not pay taxes. Taxes are necessary for the Government to operate. Recall, Government has no resources of its own. However, the Government is supposed to have a social compact (a contract with the People) with its citizens and not abuse it authority or go beyond its role of protecting our Rights. The Democrat Party, by their very own admission, wants to provide a "social" security net for citizens. On the surface, this sounds harmless and like a good idea.

A "social security net"

- social - implying togetherness and unity

- security - implying a peace of mind

- net - implying safety

The power of words! The Democrat Party is attempting to sell protection against life's adversities. However, there is not enough money in the world that will allow Government to secure you from life - Life happens! When it does, God is your "social security net." The genius of the Democrat Party is that the best way to persuade the mind (logic) is to first address the heart (emotions). Emotions kick Logic's butt everyday. On the contrary, the Republicans attempt to reach the heart through the mind. This is much more difficult because every person is emotional, but not every person is logical.

The Republicans

As mentioned several times prior, the Republican Party is not without its policy faults (capital punishment being one of the biggest - remember, the Republican Party is a temporary stopping point for Christians moving to the political-right). This being the case however, most of their policies tend to have a "spirit of trust" on the front-end of a particular action. Its policies start with the premise that mankind should first be free to choose. If, with that freedom, an individual infringes upon the Rights of others, their Rights will then be denied or removed on the back-end. However, if they use their freedoms to engage in personal vices, then he or she would address those with God. This is diagrammed in picture #23.

Picture #23

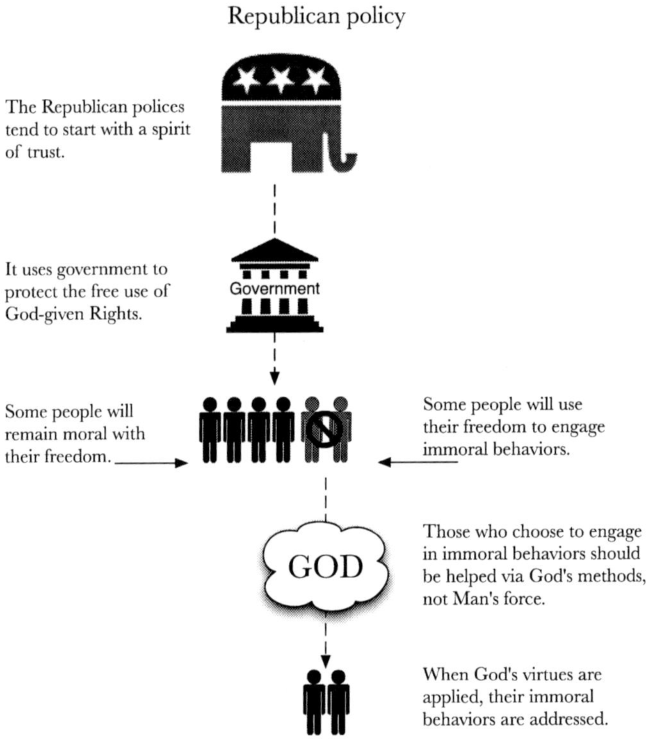

Republican policy

The Republican polices tend to start with a spirit of trust.

It uses government to protect the free use of God-given Rights.

Government

Some people will remain moral with their freedom.

Some people will use their freedom to engage immoral behaviors.

GOD

Those who choose to engage in immoral behaviors should be helped via God's methods, not Man's force.

When God's virtues are applied, their immoral behaviors are addressed.

God's love, first and foremost, allows us to be free in our actions. It is through this freedom that we can either chose to operate out of His virtues or to operate out of our vices. For example, such things as greediness, selfishness and hate are the back-end results of having the "freedom" on the front-end. The Republican policies do not advocate or promote greed, selfishness and hate. This is only perception. What you are really seeing are the symptoms of what some people will do if they are given the freedom to do so. In other words, greed, selfishness and hate are what some people choose to do with that freedom. However, if you want to ensure that absolutely no one engages in greediness, selfishness and hate, you must absolutely remove their freedoms on the "front-end." As a Christian, ensure that you are not denying or removing someone's God-given Right to be greedy, selfish or hateful by thinking you are doing them or God a favor. The very moment you enslave another adult to "your" moral authority is the moment you contradict "Christ-like" methods.

As previously mentioned, the Republican Party is far from perfect. However, the Party, as a whole, seeks to limit Government in our daily lives and that is an excellent start!

Provider or Protector?

Many Democrat entitlement programs are based upon the phrase, "the Right to Life," one of the three Rights listed within the Declaration of Independence (life, liberty and the pursuit of happiness). However, the Right to life (which is the God-given Right to be born and not murdered afterwards) and the Right to livelihood (entitlements for the necessities of life) are entirely different. Government was created to protect Rights. Therefore, it is obvious that it cannot protect the Right to personal property while at the same time redistributing that property as a means to provide for the livelihood of its citizens. Also, recall that Government is a secondary power, which gets its power from the People. The concept of a smaller portion of power being the provider of needs for the source from which it came (the People) is not possible nor exists anywhere in nature. Simply, there is no God-given Rights to livelihood. Such beliefs imply that you have a God-given Right for someone else to labor for your needs.

The ideological split of the Democrat and Republican parties can be traced to two words - provider and protector. The Democrat policies tend to "protect the livelihood" of its citizens by "providing for their needs." Such policies transfer accountability, responsibility and power from the People (primary power) to the Government (secondary power). If someone is unable to provide for their own needs, then they must petition the politician for Government rations.

The Republican policies tend to "protect the Rights" of its citizens, so they can better "provide for their own livelihood." Such policies keep the accountability, responsibility and power in the hands of the People (primary power). If someone is unable to provide for their own needs, then they should be helped through charity (God's-way of us helping others).

Government cannot be both the provider of the People and the protector of their Rights. In order to provide, Rights must be removed. It must decide on one or the other. Once the role of Government moves from protector to provider, society moves from freedom to enslavement, respectively. Since God has given us Rights, then it would make sense that the things God has given us should be protected over what Government provides for us. However, if you are casting your vote for the political party that appeals to your emotions of "helping the people," then expect to lose the very Rights God has given you as the result. God did not give you power and Rights only for you to hand them over to others.

Takeaways:

- Democrat policies tend to have an initial "spirit of distrust."

- Republican policies tend to have an initial "spirit of trust."

- God has an initial "spirit of trust."

- There is a God-given Right to life, not livelihood.

- Do not deny freedom as a cure to prevent vices.

Do not measure political parties by what they say or do not say, but rather by how their policies align with the "methods" of Christ. When you attempt to utilize Government to socially engineer a society, you must also appoint Government "masters and providers" over the People to oversee the progress. You must also remove or limit the Rights of the individual in the process. You cannot allow individuals to freely exercise their Rights while at the same time dictating the outcome of their life. Both Government and the individual cannot both share in the decision making process to determine a particular outcome. Nowhere in God's nature can this concept exist.

CHAPTER 17

VIRTUE OR VICE?

"Only a virtuous people are capable of freedom."
~ Benjamin Franklin

Virtue - moral excellence; goodness; righteousness.
Vice - immoral conduct; depraved or degrading behavior

Based on the above definitions of virtues and vices, it is quite apparent that virtues come from God and vices are acts of mankind. We know this because God is the source of morality and all things that are good, while Man is imperfect and incapable of sustaining moral excellence for long extended periods of time. Since virtues and vices represent moral and immoral conduct, respectively, they are opposites of each other. They cannot occupy the very same space at the very same time. Since Man's-government only operates out of vices, this is more proof that it is opposite of God. Therefore, it is important that Man's-government remains limited. The last thing we need is something that is opposite of God growing in size. Thus, when you limit Government, you indirectly limit its vices. Once this happens, virtues (morality) starts coming back into society. One way to limit Government reach is by filling Government positions with virtuous (morally upright) people. However, those people must understand that they are there to protect Rights, not dictate morality. As the Constitution serves to keep "external" controls on Man's-government, virtuous people within Government positions would serve to keep "internal" controls on it.

As political parties move toward the left on the political spectrum, they naturally attempt to "socially engineer" the People, trying to use laws as ways to force them towards either moral behavior. Such examples can be found within hate crime laws, "sin" taxes, anti-gouging price laws and government-forced sensitivity classes. Again, all done with good intentions, but accomplished by suppressing and enslaving the human spirit. However, people cannot be forced towards morality. This is because people cannot be forced towards God. Also, vices cannot be used to turn other vices into virtues (a negative plus a negative equals a negative). In other words, the vices of Government cannot cure the vices of Man and move him towards morality, no matter how much power and resources the People consent to giving it. The only way to move someone back towards God's virtues is to help reconnect them with their belief in a "higher power." The more an individual operates out of virtues, the closer to God they naturally become.

The reason why Christians can't be Democrats is because the Democrat Party, and those parties politically-left, tend to use Government as a means to force morality upon its citizens, hoping to create a more equal and fair society. Their policies regulate and dictate businesses, healthcare, our diets, working conditions, greed, charitable giving, parenting, fairness, job hiring, minimum wage, etc. Basically, it is Government's attempt to save us from ourselves. In defense to the Democrat Party, this does not imply that the Republicans do not use regulations; it is just that Democrats tend to call for more regulations. The problem with using laws and regulations to create morality is that it cannot be done effectively. This is because "forced morality" is an oxymoron. Such laws and regulations will seem to work at first, because people are forced to comply. However, forcing the human spirit goes against our innate feeling of wanting to be free. Giving Government the responsibility of creating virtuous citizens is like giving Satan the responsibility of churning out God-fearing people. It simply cannot be done. No matter how many programs, regulations, laws and sin taxes Government creates, it cannot ever be successful. Since virtues come from God, not from Government, only God is the true way to moral citizens and a virtuous society. The very same God that Government has previously separated itself from.

Virtues play a huge part in American freedom. This is because the more morally upright we are, the less we need Government to intervene. However, improving morality is the responsibility of the individual, not the Government. Fortunately for us, God has placed virtues in our God-basket. Start applying the virtue that is opposite of the vice that you would like to conquer. (perform an Internet search of "virtues and vices" to get a comprehensive list). Recall that virtues are in God's basket, not Government's. This means that Government is ill equipped to fix the vices of its citizens. Unfortunately though, every political party that currently exists has either used the concept of morality to either deny or remove someone's God-given Rights or have called for laws that would "legalize" immorality:

- Political far left - there is no general belief in God, thus nothing truly comes from God, because He is nonexistent. Therefore, all things flow top-down from Government, making the People inferior. Rights are determined by Government.

- Political left - is comprised of voters who believe in God and some who do not. The party is far from being "equally yoked." This borders the "half-way" point where society starts to shift from the belief in God to not believing. This is where we should *not* be as Christians. Because of the political-left's beliefs in social equality, fairness and entitlements, some God-given Rights are removed.

- Political right - like the political left, it is comprised of voters who believe in God and some who do not. There is a general belief that God's-government is above Man's-government, therefore goodness is able to flow top-down from God to the People. The role of Man's-government, which is inferior to the People, is to protect the Rights and endowments from God. However, some on the far political-right do use their moral beliefs as a way to deny certain Rights.

Takeaways:

- Use virtues to fix vices; however, vices can only break virtues.

- God "heals" mankind, not "sin" taxes.

- A morally upright society is a free society, because it requires less Man's-government.

Our form of government in the United States only works well with people who are virtuous (morally upright). Without virtues, people cannot properly self-govern themselves. Being forcefully governed by others is a form of enslavement, which is opposite of freedom. So, the more society is able to govern itself, the more free it becomes. Thus, we must solve problems using virtues, not vices. God wants us to use His virtues as a way of digging ourselves out of our immoral behaviors and as a way of help others address theirs. Do not be so quick to replace God's ways with Government. You will only be trading out virtues for vices (morality for immorality).

CHAPTER 18

SO, WHAT'S A CHRISTIAN TO DO?

"Duty is ours; results are God's" ~ *John Quincy Adams*

Although our nation is currently in moral decay, it is not too late to turn things around. There is no particular order that you must do things in. Just do whatever you can whenever you can do it. Just ensure that you do something! Fortunately, God has already given us the answers to our problems. They are found within his virtues and commandments. Just remember that when following one commandment, be sure not to break another. For example, you cannot follow the commandment of compassion while knowingly breaking the commandment not to steal. He is not a God of contradiction. Unfortunately, our greatest challenge is having enough faith in believing God's ways will work. Humans beings are practical being - we recognize visual results. This is where faith comes in. Faith requires having a conviction in those things not seen.

One variation of the "freedom formula (G-f=F)" states that when force is removed from in-between you and God, His blessings are able to flow down unobstructed. Therefore, have faith that when we reduce the overall influence of Man's-government in society that God's-government will reenter. When you reduce Government, the power it previously held is restored to you. With this newfound power, you are now able to help more people. In addition, you also regain your financial resources it previously held in its tax coffers. As with power, you are now able to share your financial blessing with others too. Recall in the "133 crayons experiment" (chapter 4) that solutions and innovations are more abundant when people are able to freely use their God-given talents and resources. This implies that the cure to various diseases and the solutions to other problems will come about much faster when Man's-government gets out of the way of the process. Forced equality, at the cost of regulating the human spirit, will always stifle creativity and technological advancements. Again, this is not to say that Man's-government should be %100 absent in certain situations, but only reduced to its lowest level of necessary involvement. Once it is, the ways of God will have "room to work."

Voting

Using the power of your vote is one of the easiest things you can do to start restoring God's-government in society. Recall that Man's-government is completely opposite of God's-government. Therefore, the very moment you vote for the political party that sincerely seeks to "reduce" Man's-government in our daily lives, is the moment you start the shift back towards God and His love, abundance, morality and independence. Your vote sends a clear message to Government that you reject its dependency and enslavement and reestablishes your renewed faith that God's way will prevail in healing the ills of the world. This is what He promised us. This is a natural principle found throughout His universe.

One of the greatest challenges will be voting for another political party that does not, on the surface, represent what you believe to be of God. This will be a great test of your faith. Remember however, you are not voting for the specific men and women that are representing that party. You are voting for the party whose ideologies seek to reduce Man's-government in our lives. Vote for those candidates who understand their role in government and are able to verbalize it when questioned. Their role is to protect those things of God, not redistribute them. Besides, how can they effectively perform their job if they don't know what it is? If they cannot explain the very basic of their job responsibility in ten words or less ("to protect the unalienable rights from God …"), chances are that they will fail in their duty or overextend it. We must vote for those candidates that seek to repeal unjust laws. Any man-law that regulates a God-law or removes a God-given Right at the expense of a privilege is unjust. Before you determine which candidate(s) you might align yourself with, first consider which candidates you should not be aligned with. This will make the choice much easier. Have an understanding of God's underlying principles first. Recall, it not necessarily what would Jesus do, but how He would have done it. If the candidate is not aligned with God's principles then you may want to seek another candidate. Understand that it will take several political election cycles to reverse the course of our country. Remain steadfast in your vote and God's universal principles will take hold. We can make an immediate shift in America simply by voting "God's-government" during the next election.

Education

Freedom is not earned, but learned. Everyone must do something, but this does not mean that one person must do everything. There are many things that you can choose to get involved with that will change the course of our nation. To make an impact, we need educators, organizers and those willing to "sell and tell" the "freedom formula" to the masses. Every Christian needs to do their part on educating others on the legitimate role of Man's-government and its relationship with God. Your knowledge is your obligation to share, therefore:

- Educate yourself on how the political process works in the United States.

- Educate yourself on the process of how laws are created.

- Educate yourself on the proper roles of the three branches of government – the executive, legislative and the judicial. The three branches were created to separate power, not combine it.

- Educate yourself on our government of federalism, which separates power vertically across various levels of government and the People.

- Educate others on the differences between God-given Rights and Man/Government privileges.

- Study the Declaration of Independence and the US Constitution. The former spells out how freedom works and the latter helps secure (protect) that freedom. They are inseparable.

- Educate others by having conversations about the difference between God's-government and Man's-government. Remember, discussing one without the other is a disservice to all.

- Organize and host various groups and discussion that speak on the topic of government, not necessarily politics.

- Get involved in your local school system. Our educators, entrusted with educating our children, do not understand where Rights come from or the role of government or the purpose of the Declaration of Independence and US Constitution. Schools are secondary powers. Therefore, it is important that you delegate to your local school board, rather having them delegate to you.

- Teach the "Freedom Formula (G-g=F)" everywhere you go.

Note - there will be ongoing discussions, articles and resources on the "Why Christians can't be Democrat" website:

Website: www.whychristianscantbedemocrats.com

Communities

Over the years, whole communities have built up a dependency upon the Government. They have literally transferred so much responsibility and power to Government that even if they wanted to reclaim it, they do not even have enough power to do so. Governments have always been hesitant to return power to the People. Communities must start weaning themselves off of entitlement programs. While doing so, we must step up and help them through compassion and charity. This is what we are commanded to do. This has to be a total effort, from within and outside such communities. We must help those who want to remove themselves from the dependency of Man, so they can move back under God. Communities are declining because the People are willingly transferring their power, not because it is being forcefully taken from them. They are seeking help via Man-ways, instead of the ways of God. We need to start growing the power of individuals. They too must wean themselves off of government. There is no such thing as an independent dependent. This requires education of principles, finances and self-responsibility. Refrain from using your vote to "enable" such communities. Vote against the politician that wants to do that work of God byway of their Government position. Share your blessings with those within these communities. Personal dignity will be the result of both the giver and the receiver. Encourage those within your community to exercise their own power to make change. This step alone would start the universal shift from enslavement to freedom and abundance. Whatever you do, absolutely do NOT enlist Government's assistance to help you rid yourself of Government.

Christian Challenges

It is your Christian duty to "plug in" somewhere in the process. Again, take some time to understand our political system, get involved with education or government service at some level and encourage the "freedom formula" with those within your place of worship. Unfortunately, there will be plenty of people that will choose to completely reject or remain silent in educating their congregation or fellow Christians on the concept of Man's-government. Their Christian arrogance will only permit them to discuss God-government, which is only half of the "freedom formula." They will never be fully exposed to the complete formula, thus they will only be half-armed in the battle. There will be churches that will refrain from speaking directly against those political parties that promote the expansion of Man's-government from fear of losing their Government 501(c)(3) tax benefits. They would rather reap the financial benefits of Man's-government than speak against it.

Christians should move back to the political-right, towards God. We are not equally yoked with those political parties that reside politically-left. There is something obviously wrong when you have "Christians" spread across the whole political spectrum. How can we say we are yoked in being "Christ-like" while at the same time unyoked in our beliefs in Man's-government? As we move to the political-right, we need to respect the 1st Amendment and refrain from using Government to force our God's-government beliefs on others.

As Christians, we have a duty to uplift the will of God by enacting the methods of Christ. We, too, have an obligation to protect those things that God has given. We must secure our "God-basket." When we all work to reduce the influence of Man's-government in society, it will start to heal. All of the things of God will return. Such things as independence, morality, compassion, love and stronger family units will come back into our homes and communities. Jobs and finances will be in abundance. If we want communities to get better, we must put government back in its position of servitude, beneath the People, not in-between the People and God. The world cannot get better as long as we allow Man to limit the God-given abilities and talents of all because we cannot trust the actions of some. God has called upon us to use His ways of dealing with social ills. This means that when faced with such challenges, we are to utilize those items within His basket, not the basket of Man's-government. History has proven to us that the institution of Man's-Government does a very good job when it comes to force and destruction. This is the very nature of its design and purpose - to use various methods of force and destruction to ensure that no one, no State or no other country infringes upon the Rights of other citizens, other States or the United States as a whole. This being the case, it does not make sense to invite Man's-government to the solution table to discuss ideas of how to solve problems or how to provide for its citizens. This is the purpose of God's-government. Man's-government should only attend such meetings in the capacity of sergeant of arms.

"Why Christians can't be Democrats" serves as a "government" handbook for the Christian voter. Use it as one of your guides to reclaim God's freedom for America. Remember, such freedoms will not happen without your actions. However, if you choose to stay on the sidelines, understand that it does not mean the battle between Man and God is not being waged. Now, take a look at the list you wrote that states what God is to you. The very things on this list are reduced each time force pushes God out of society. Man's-government is not the keeper of your personal Christian duties and responsibilities. Grab your "God-basket" and get to work! The duty is yours.

REFERENCES

Chapter 2

1. "The Original Declaration model" - image used by permission and courtesy of Joseph Andrews (A Guide for Learning and Teaching the Declaration of Independence and the US Constitution)

2. "The Current Declaration model" - image used by permission and courtesy of Joseph Andrews (A Guide for Learning and Teaching the Declaration of Independence and the US Constitution)

Chapter 5
1. The concept of indigenous and surrogate power attributed to Glenda Green - Love Without End: Jesus Speaks, Spiritis Publishing (January 1, 1999)